Praise for Conscious Change Today

~ International Awards ~

Book Excellence Award ~ Inspirational Category
Living Now Award ~ Femininity Category
San Francisco Book Festival ~ General Non-Fiction
San Francisco Book Festival ~ Spirituality Category
Amazon #1 New Release

Impressively informative, exceptionally thoughtful and thought-provoking, remarkably 'reader friendly' in organization and presentation. "Conscious Change Today: From Me to We ~ COVID, Climate Change, and the Rise of Feminine-Energy" is an extraordinary and timely study that is especially and unreservedly recommended for the personal reading lists of students, academia, feminists, and non-specialist general readers; and also community and college/university library Contemporary Philosophy collections in general, and Feminism supplemental curriculum studies lists in particular.

Helen Dumont ~ *Midwest Book Review*

What Kashonia Carnegie Ph.D. presented was ever-fascinating, demanding that I think more deeply about everything. And I did. There is just so much I could tell you about Conscious Change Today but I could never do Kashonia Carnegie justice if I did that. You need to read this book for yourself. You need to understand why and how the transformation in our thinking can and must occur.

Viga Boland ~ *Readers' Favorite*

"... your message is extremely timely"
Justine Willis-Toms ~ *New Dimensions Radio*

I thought that Conscious Change Today by Kashonia Carnegie Ph.D. was extremely fascinating with so many things I loved. I loved how she used world news events to explain her data. I also loved that she shared her story because I was able to relate. Kashonia Carnegie gave some really neat activities, which give you something to ponder. I loved that she discussed both sides, not just one side. I loved the websites she gave as well, and she was not spammy like some people so that was refreshing. The charts were helpful too. I also loved that she did not get too preachy, as some of these books do. If you have been interested in the conscious movement or interested in the meaning of numbers, this is a well thought out book to help you.

Renee Guill ~ *Readers' Favorite*

Initially I thought this book would be anti-male but the topic of the rise of feminine energy, particularly since 2000, was handled very well with the emphasis on equality. Dr Carnegie also shows a balanced concern about the 'MeToo' phenomena. I found the book thought-provoking, well-constructed, and an easy inspirational read with many glimpses of the author's dry sense of humor.

Ward Young ~ *freelance magazine writer and author*

I found Conscious Change Today to be a refreshing look at what feminism is for the generation that is next in line to inherit the planet. Where Dr. Carnegie sets herself apart from other books on the topic is in the spiritual approach taken, reaching past the mainstream observance of feminism and instead exploring the sacred, metaphysical philosophy that few take the time to undertake. Carnegie also very bravely discusses how the #MeToo movement applied to her in the most terrifying way, using her personal experience to fill the gaps that represent the worst of a patriarchal society and fairly smooth over the balance that has been too long in the making.

Asher Syed ~ *Readers' Favorite Reviews*

Download Your FREE E-Book Now

Conscious Leader's Guide to …
Living a Meaningful Life ~ Making a Difference

Discover how making a difference to others will make a difference to your own life by giving your life meaning.

Just go to the following Link
www.ConsciousChangeToday.com/subscribe/

THE CONSCIOUS CHANGE SERIES OF BOOKS
BY KASHONIA CARNEGIE PHD
(All due out by early-2021)

Conscious Change Today: *From Me to We ~ COVID, Climate Change, and the Rise of Feminine Energy*

Conscious Intelligence Competencies: *Taking Emotional Intelligence to the Next Level for Our 21st Century World of Relationships ~ with Yourself and Others, in Business, with the Planet, and Beyond*

Conscious Self-Discovery: *Enriching Your Relationship with Yourself*

Conscious Love: *Cultivating a Consciousness of Virtue-Based Love-in-Action for a Peaceful, Loving, and Sustainable World*

Conscious Environmental Sustainability: *Saving Our Planet through the LOVE of Nature, instead of the FEAR of Climate Change*

Conscious Economic Sustainability: *Equality and an Ethically Sustainable Financial System in Our Post-COVID World*

Conscious Social Sustainability

Conscious Democracy

WEBSITE: www.ConsciousChangeToday.com

Conscious Change Today

**From Me to We ~
COVID, Climate Change,
and the
Rise of Feminine-Energy**

Discover the link between our
changing world, the rise in the
status of women, equality,
COVID, and Climate Change

2020

Conscious Change Today: From Me to We ~ COVID, Climate Change, and the Rise of Feminine Energy

Published by: https://www.ConsciousChangeToday.com

Cover Design: Geoff Affleck (Self-publishing Consultant) & pro_ebookcovers

Cover Photo: La luna sopra l'acqua by Detelina Petkova
http://www.detelinapetkova.com

Two key symbols of the feminine include the moon and the water. And so the rising moon over the water is a perfect representation of our rising feminine-energy. Swirls, curves, and circles as seen in the title and author font are also symbolic of the feminine.

Paperback: ISBN: 978-0-6487616-1-7
e-Book: ISBN: 978-0-6487616-2-4

The author and her agents assume no responsibility for errors or omissions and expressly disclaim any responsibility for any liability, loss, or risk, personal or otherwise, which is incurred as a consequence, directly or indirectly, of the use and application of any of the contents of this book. You are required to read the "Important Notes for Readers," which can be found after the Table of Contents.

Dedicated to

Dedicated to those very special young people born around the year 2000 +/-. ~ Our Gen Zs.

You are the ones who were born to really make a difference to this world of ours.

Know that you are supported by the consciousness of over 7 billion people, even though they don't realise it.

Conscious Change Today
Description

THE UNRECOGNISED LINK BETWEEN COVID, CLIMATE CHANGE, & WOMEN'S EMPOWERMENT

Conscious Change is about moving **from *Me to We*.** And the **Conscious Change Movement** is **growing every day** leading to **greater happiness, success,** and **a meaningful life,** plus **a more peaceful, loving,** and **sustainable world.**

Both COVID and Climate Change have a common source—environmentally unsustainable practices based on outdated, unethical "Me" attitudes. The solution can be found in the rise in a caring feminine-energy-based conscious "We" culture.

The dominating Me attitude, characteristic of the number 1, prevailed throughout the last 1000 years—**1**000+/--**1**999+/-. With the arrival of the **2**000s a new, ethical, feminine-We focus dawned that "coincidentally" has been characteristic of the number 2 for thousands of years.

Supported by the quantum theory of global consciousness focusing on our new **2**000 millennium, it is positive feminine-We-2 energy at this time that I demonstrate is arguably behind the rise in the status of women.

And this new feminine-We-2 attitude is saying enough is enough to the Me-1 mindset with its dominating, bully-boy tactics, and frequently in many areas, corruption.

Although more commonly found in women, the adoption of this conscious We-2 feminine-energy is essential for both men and women now our new 2000-millennium is with us. It's interesting to see the increasing acceptance of the new, softer, 2020-We version of Joe Biden, versus the negative, outdated Me focused Donald Trump.

Most scientists agree that if you dig down, COVID is ultimately caused by the unsustainable destruction of habitat and biodiversity due to some form of human development—built or agricultural—very Me activities.

So native wildlife, who carry these viruses, have had to come in closer and closer contact with humans. The same unsustainable humanisation of our natural world is also the basis of climate change.

Underpinning all this environmental destruction is our unsustainable growth economy—also a very outdated Me focused system. A system that began nearly 100 years ago as a temporary measure yet is still with us today. Just imagine if we continued to rely on a 100-year-old transportation or communication system.

Is COVID just a very mild practice run for Climate Change that will make COVID seem like child's play, both socially and economically?

We need the open-minded courage to acknowledge the consequences of our past actions that we're having to live with today. For our world to change it's vital that we move from our negative, last-millennium Me culture to an ethical 2000-We attitude.

Indeed, our ever growing 2020-We culture is demanding a Conscious Change Today. We ignore that Me to We change, at our peril.

Table of Contents

PART 2 ~ Living a Conscious Life Today

Activities

Important Notes to Readers

USE OF "YOU"

Occasionally I use the 2nd person pronoun "you" in a generic 3rd person way, not because it necessarily applies to you specifically. So please don't take offence.

If this was an academic paper, I'd probably be using "one" as the 3rd person pronoun. For instance, one might say this or one might do that. But I can't tell you how much this one hates that sort of language.

AUSTRALIAN ENGLISH

This book is written in an Australian/UK English. So if you're from a non-Commonwealth country, I hope you don't find it too distracting.

DISCLAIMER

All humans are very different and think and react in different ways to different things. And so if anything in this book raises any issues or concerns for you it's important that you talk with a good psychological health care professional.

Yours Free !!!

Global Conscious Change is taking us out of the dark and into the sunshine. And so I invite you to visit my Conscious Change Today website and fill in the opt-in form so I can keep you informed of forthcoming Conscious Change publications and workshops, and the latest Conscious (change the world) news.

You'll also receive a free copy of my *Conscious Leader's Guide to ~ Living a Meaningful Life ~ Making a Difference*

Just go to

https://www.ConsciousChangeToday.com/subscribe

And a Favour ???

If you think the messages in this book are important please tell your friends about the book and spread the word to all on your mailing lists, blogs, and social media feeds.

And because Amazon's decision to promote a book is largely based on reviews, if you're an Amazon customer, I'd really appreciate you leaving a review on the book's Amazon page. Just go to

https://tinyurl.com/ConsciousChangeToday

Thank You So Much.

~ Chapter 1 ~
Conscious Change is Coming~
But It's Up to You

The beginning is always today.
~ **Mary Wollstonecraft** ~

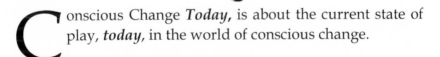

Conscious Change *Today,* is about the current state of play, *today*, in the world of conscious change.

Yet it's also a reminder that:
>The Time is Now,
>It's Up to You,
>The Choice is Yours ~

You CAN make a Conscious Change, *Today.*

The term "conscious" was first introduced into the business literature in 2002 with the first edition of Fred Kofman's book, *Conscious Business: How to Build Value through Values.* A major change then occurred in 2005 when Patricia

Aburdene, known for co-authoring a number of *Megatrends* books with John Naisbitt, published her best-selling book, *Megatrends 2010: The Rise of Conscious Capitalism*. This was closely followed, in 2006, by the very extensive and much-heralded blog post *"Conscious Capitalism: Creating a New Paradigm for Business"*, written by John Mackey, the co-founder and CEO of Whole Foods Market.

The "conscious" flame had been ignited.

Globally, today we're experiencing a conscious revolution with a focus on areas such as conscious business, conscious leadership, conscious parenting, conscious consumerism, and the list goes on.

Can it really be purely coincidental that this *conscious revolution* began with the arrival of our new millennium—the year 2000+/- with, as you'll discover in the coming pages, its focus on acting in ethical, loving, and virtuous ways.

But what is this "conscious" change really all about?

The word conscious, is generally thought to mean having an awareness or being aware. But being aware of what? And this is rarely clearly defined in the current range of books focusing on the ever-growing conscious movement.

And without a strong firm definition, it's hard to focus on what's really important.

Is conscious business just about being aware of business skills? Is conscious parenting just about being aware of parenting skills? And is conscious change just being aware of change? No, no, and no.

When conscious is used in that manner it's all about digging much deeper than just the descriptor—business, or parenting, or change, or whatever. It's about taking the conscious part to a far deeper level than just "being aware".

In essence, in the context of the current use of the word "conscious"; working in a conscious way or living a conscious life is about having an awareness of our world and how everything and everyone is interrelated, interdependent, and so everything impacts on everything else. As a result, it's about how we can best act to enhance and ensure the flourishing of all in and on our world — human and non-human, animate and so-called inanimate alike. This is explained in a lot more detail in Competency 4 in *Conscious Intelligence Competencies: Taking Emotional Intelligence to the Next Level for Our 21st Century World of Relationships…*

Conscious and so conscious change is about ensuring that the decisions we make and the actions we take have an ethical foundation — are about *we not me.* This usually has an added dash of quantum spirituality to assist in making those decisions.

Sounds simple, but there's also more to the notion of ethics than meets the eye.

As an ethicist, over the years I've discovered that most people want to act in an ethical manner. And most people think that they do act in an ethical manner. But believe me, that's not always the case.

All too many people will do whatever it takes, no matter who gets hurt, in their bid to get what *they* want — *me* **not** *we.*

It's commonplace for people to chase ever greater financial riches and what they perceive as the power it will bring them, no matter what. It's all about *me not we.*

And are you aware that research shows that around 50% +/- of people grew up in some form of dysfunctional family? A dysfunctional family that focuses on *me not we.*

Take my own case. I used to think I had a good childhood because I was always fed, clothed, given a private school education, and never sexually or physically abused, other than the odd slap across the bottom.

Then decades later when I began to study the area of psychological child abuse, I realised that out of 32 ways children can be psychologically abused, I grew up with 12 of them.

To begin with, it was a loveless home. Indeed the word "LOVE" was considered a four-letter word not to be mentioned, unless referring to your favourite food. No one ever told anyone that they were loved.

And as all too many people have experienced, throughout my entire childhood I was constantly told how great a disappointment I was to my parents that I was born a girl and not a boy. It's also common for boys to be an equal disappointment to their parents because they aren't girls.

But I was repeatedly told that my name was meant to be Stephen Charles. So my parents made the best of a bad situation and although I was christened Stephanie, I was always called Stevie.

My parents weren't necessarily bad people, but their focus was always on what *they* wanted and expected without any consideration of its impact on others – *me not we.*

And it's not unusual for those who've grown up in a dysfunctional home as a child, to end up in a dysfunctional marriage and be the victim, and hopefully survivor, of domestic violence.

The World Health Organisation figures indicate that around one in three women experience sexual or physical violence at the hand of their intimate partner. But the incidence of psychological abuse is far, far greater than physical abuse. Some estimates are around the 70% mark.

And yes, I was one of those too.

During a three-year marriage in my late twenties, I nearly lost my life on three separate occasions.

Once, as I ran up my suburban street dodging gun fire I was continually thanking *Starsky and Hutch* for teaching me to run in a zig-zagging fashion if ever bullets are heading my way.

Another time was due to severe internal haemorrhaging. And the third occasion was when my husband at the time attempted to drown me in the surf so that he could claim the half a million dollars in insurance money that he'd taken out on my life.

However, and you might find this hard to believe, but far worse than those near-death experiences, was the brainwashing. The daily psychological abuse that was so insidious that I didn't even realise it was happening until many years after I (literally) escaped from the marriage.

And what's domestic violence all about—physical, sexual, or psychological? It's about one partner, more commonly the man but not always, wanting what *they* want—*me not we*.

And on it goes.

The use of illicit drugs for feel good gratification, no matter how many people get hurt along the way is all about *me not we*.

I'm sure there's hardly a person around who hasn't been stung by some form of unethical business practice or scam—*me not we*.

And there can be no forgetting the good old "selfie" ~ look at me everyone. It doesn't normally hurt people but what a great demonstration of our current *me not we* culture. It can also be an indication of something much deeper, such as a desperate seeking for approval and love. Why are they so desperately in need of that approval and love?

So in its very simplest form, Conscious Change is all about changing a "me" focus to a "we" focus—*from me to we.*

Generally speaking, those who have experienced abuse or a traumatic experience will come out the other side primarily in one of three ways.

1. They'll end up withdrawn, and in need of some good professional help.

2. They'll be filled with hate and vengeance, as I'll talk about later in the book.

3. Or they'll be filled with an overwhelming need to get out there and make a difference to the world.

My deep passion for conscious change has come from my painful past combined with being endowed with the gift of number 3 — an overwhelming need to get out there and make a difference to the world.

My Passion for Conscious Change

Recently I watched the semi-finals of the TV show, *The Voice*. And this year more than any other I was amazed at the quality of the voices of virtually all the contestants. Any one of them could have equalled almost any paid professional singer.

But as one of the judges said, it was no longer about vocal quality. What he was looking for was the passion, the truth, the authenticity, the vulnerability, that was embedded in the presentation of the song. Something that has to come from the heart and the soul, not the voice-box.

And on semi-final night one of the contestants just knocked me right over because he touched me so deeply with his passion and sincerity.

His name is Johnny Manuel, an openly gay man of colour who found the love of his life in Australia, where he now lives despite being born and growing up in the United States.

The song he sang was Sam Cooke's, 1964 anthem, *A Change Is Gonna Come*. As you're probably aware, it was originally written as a protest song to support the civil rights movement, after Sam and his team were turned away from a whites-only motel in Louisiana.

The next day I spent quite some time trying to work out why, a very white little Aussie-girl, well okay — woman of more mature years — like me would be so moved by the song.

Was it the fact that at this time with all that's going on in the world, from Black Lives Matter, to #MeToo, COVID, and Climate Change that the world is in such great need of change in so many areas that I'm so passionate about?

Or was it purely Johnny's heart-felt passion that jumped right out of my television screen and embraced me with such warmth assuring me that change was indeed coming as the last line of the song promises — "I know a change's gonna come, oh yes, it will"?

Or was it that I resonated so deeply with Johnny's words just before he took to the stage? He said with such heartfelt dedication: "I know inside of myself that I was put here to do this".

I've said those same words about my *Conscious Change* Series of Books. "I know inside of myself that I was put here, and more importantly experienced the life I have, to write these books on ethics-based change". And every day the Universe sends me more and more evidence that that belief is true. Such as Johnny Manuel's magic performance of *A Change Is Gonna Come*.

I think it was a combination of all those things because Johnny's whole segment, which I've now watched many times, made me realise the genuine depth of my passion for this topic of Conscious Change in a brand-new way. Just like the depth of the passion that that American gay man of colour had when he sang that song.

What that performance did was to take me out of my normal, very safe, intellectual passion for conscious change, and it moved me to my deepest possible vulnerable heart and soul-based passion for conscious change and what I'm doing. And I made some very significant changes as a result[1].

On many occasions I've said to people "I know a change's gonna come, oh yes, it will". Or words to that effect. And on so many occasions the response has been laughter, or something like "dream on girl".

When talking and writing about change on all levels — *conscious* change/ethics-based change — I often preface what I'm about to say by asking my readers or listeners to believe in unicorns. And I add, more and more unicorns are definitely showing up every day. And they are!

I invite you too to just watch out for the unicorns — the metaphorical, as well as the physical ones in the form of toys, pictures, and scarfs. I even have a unicorn-print cloth COVID face-mask. And there's a relatively new TV sit-com called The Unicorn. They really are appearing everywhere.

But there's another major reason why I am so passionate about Conscious Change. As you're aware if you read the first few pages, I know what life is like when it's not around, when people are *me* focused instead of *we* focused.

Yet even far more important than that. I know that this stuff works.

In my role as Australia's first female oil company representative in the early 1970s, I instinctively used and taught what is now known as conscious leadership and conscious business practices with all of my clients. And they all experienced great business success as a result. And *their* business success also meant *my* success within the oil company. Definitely a "WE" result. This is something I talk more about in Book 2 of the Conscious Change Series of Books – *Conscious Intelligence Competencies*.

Then in the 1980s I won Australia's top radio award due to my instinctive conscious communication skills when listening to, talking with, and helping my callers. Again I was able to change the lives of everyday people by focusing on *we not me*.

Had the "conscious" buzz-word been around at the time I submitted my doctoral thesis/dissertation, *Heart-Centred Virtue Ethics: Raising Ecological Consciousness in Organisations*, I would have submitted it in the field of the ethics of conscious change.

And so naturally those same conscious business and conscious leadership skills were the same skills I taught to my MBA leadership students in the late 1990s and on into the 2000s.

I often recall a student from one of my Hong Kong, MBA Leadership classes — I'll call him Chen. He was an accountant in his late thirties and held a responsible position in the company where he worked. And like most of my Hong Kong students, he was Chinese.

These classes were always taught over two face-to-face long weekends, a month apart, and the rest virtually via email. The first weekend I'd teach the class the essence of what I now refer to as Conscious Intelligence Competencies. These competencies include empathy, self-awareness, and how everything we do and say is interrelated — Everything impacts on everything else. These are essential skills and understandings for every business leader.

During the second weekend of Chen's class I'd just finished reviewing these topics and we'd gone to a break when Chen came up to me.

He had tears in his eyes, which began to bubble over and run down his cheeks as he began to speak.

"Dr. Kashonia, I want to thank you for teaching us about such things. I'm 38 years old and never have I even heard of these topics, much less learned about them. After last weekend, I put some of the things you taught us into practice with my life at home with my family. We were going through a rough spot, and what you taught us completely changed all of our lives. Why have I never learned these skills before now?"

By this time, I too was nearly crying and I said how wonderful it was that he was benefiting so much from the class. What an amazingly beautiful gift that was for me to receive.

But it wasn't a one-off gift. As had happened with my radio listeners, students would often let me know how they implemented a model or a process that they'd learned about in class. And they'd go on to explain how it was working fantastically well for them, changing their lives either at home or at work, or both.

Oh and two and a half thousand years ago the Greek philosopher, Aristotle, was teaching what could arguably be called a form of conscious conduct. So it's nothing new. It just needed a bit of dusting off and updating.

As you can see, Conscious Change and Conscious Intelligence Competencies work! And it works just as successfully within the family, the community, business, and society at large.

But for the greatest global success, we all need to work together to bring about that conscious change, as you'll discover as you journey through the following pages.

~ Chapter 2 ~
From Me to We & The Caveat

*I know that as more and more people choose to embark
on this Me to We journey, our actions in turn
encourage others to do the same.*

~ Craig Kielburger ~

☯

The dominating "Me" attitude, characteristic of the number 1, prevailed throughout the last 1000 years. With the arrival of the 2000s a new, ethical "We" focus dawned that "coincidentally" for thousands of years has been characteristic of the number 2. This new We attitude is saying enough is enough to the Me mindset with its dominating, bully-boy tactics, and frequently in some areas, corruption.

Although more commonly found in women, this positive We feminine-2-energy is essential for both men and women to adopt now our new 2000-millennium is with us. It was interesting to see the increasing acceptance of the new, softer, 2020-We version of Joe Biden, versus the very negative, outdated Me focused Donald Trump.

We all need the open-minded courage to acknowledge the consequences of our past actions that we're living with today. For our world to change it's vital that we move from the negative, last-millennium Me culture to an ethical We attitude. Our ever growing 2020 We culture is demanding a conscious change today and we ignore that change, from Me to We, at our peril.

The English evolutionary biologist, Richard Dawkins, has been criticized for many of his more philosophical views, but my main criticism of his work is the misleading title that he gave to the book that brought him to world prominence in 1976. The book is called, *The Selfish Gene*.

Most people just assume that he's arguing that humans are born selfish, when he's actually arguing the reverse. As he says, selection has favoured genes that **cooperate** with each other. And so they are selfish only in as much as they realise that if they don't **contribute** to the greater good of those genes beyond themselves, they will die. This is why the common definition of living a meaningful life is to contribute to some-thing or some-one outside of ourselves, "beyond ourselves" — *we* **not** *me*.

In philosophy, one of the arguments about a genuine egoist, which can appear to be very confusing, is that they often act in a seemingly very altruistic manner. This is because they know that acting altruistically, no matter how false, is how they'll get what they want in life.

From me to we is the foundation of a successful life no matter how you define success.

A question for you!

What is it that you want most in life? What is it that you've been longing for but can't seem to attract?

Is it happiness, friendships, "the one", fame, even if it's money; throughout my Conscious Change Series of Books I'll continually demonstrate how to get any of those things by acting in a "conscious" manner.

In the meantime, the short answer is to dig, dig, dig. When you dig, dig, dig, down far enough, the ultimate solution to what you're after is to begin to focus on *we not me*. And that might sound very simplistic. And it is. It's simple although not always easy.

On the surface, the seeking of fame, for example, can be seen as an egocentric, look-at-me and start loving me endeavour. A bit like the selfie.

The 18th century Scottish moral philosopher, David Hume, who had a starring role in my doctoral thesis/dissertation, was often erroneously criticised for seeking "literary fame". Yet without that literary fame no one would have ever heard any of his great life-changing insights and wisdom.

And as Hume explained: If someone is seeking fame all that public good will be for nothing if that person is not also a good (ethical) role model. So anyone achieving, or even seeking, a high public profile should constantly reflect on everything they say and do, far more than the average person. This is to ensure they're the most ethical role-model possible. In doing this their fame will indeed be about a *we not a me* attitude.

And just one more example.

Let's take a quick look at the controversial issue of money. Is the seeking of money a *we* or a *me* thing?

There's nothing wrong with seeking money. After all in our current world we all need money to take care of ourselves along the way.

It's like you're always told on an aeroplane to make sure you put *your* oxygen mask on first if, heaven forbid, the occasion arises. Because you can't help others if you're in need of help yourself.

So when it comes to wanting money, as with any of the things you might have been wanting; again it's all about dig, dig, digging down to work out honestly *why* you want them. One of the first things you learn in NLP—Neuro-Linguistic Programming—is to always know your outcome.

It's often said that the universe doesn't want you to struggle. The universe wants you to be comfortable so you're in a better position to help others. It's hard to take care of others when you're constantly worried about being evicted from your rental house, or unable to pay your mortgage.

But there's a big difference between having a very comfortable albeit modest home, and having ten, mega-million-dollar homes scattered through the world. **Needs versus Greeds.**

I've always been very impressed with Warren Buffet. For decades he's been one of the world's richest men, yet he lives in a very modest home in Nebraska. And sure he has a beach home in California that he virtually never visits and is said to have been bought at the request of his wife—*we not me*.

Another question to dig into is: What are you prepared to do, either positive or negative, to achieve your outcome? Basically, do you want whatever it is, money, new clothes, a big house, fame, or whatever, for egocentric (ME) reasons? Or as part of your WE outcomes and plans?

So if you want to live a conscious life, make sure you're going after needs, not greeds. And be very aware, or conscious, of:

(1) why you want it—whatever it might be?

(2) How you intend to go after it?

(3) What impact, positive and/or negative, will your actions and outcomes have on others? Conscious Intelligence Competency 6 will help you here.

These are all issues I help you explore in depth in *Conscious Self-Discovery: Enriching Your Relationship with Yourself,* which is the companion book to *Conscious Intelligence Competencies.*

Johnny Manuel said he was "put here to do this" so that his message for equality can be heard by millions. Singing is how Johnny is making a difference. His singing is not about me, but about we. Writing and teaching is how I now strive to make a difference.

We all have different skills and strengths that we can hone and develop so that we can become conscious leaders of change and go out and make a difference in our world, or even the world.

Finally, before moving on to the promised caveat, I'd like to share the full quote that I adapted at the start of this chapter. It appeared on Craig Keilburger's blog in August 2019[2]. It's beautiful, very true, and very inspiring. It goes like this:

> I believe that every journey from ME to WE is as unique as each one of us, filled with twists and turns that lead in directions we might never have expected. I know that as more and more people choose to embark on this journey, our actions in turn encourage others to find their own routes. When I think about the future, I imagine all of our paths converging forging a new direction for our society. As I look around today I can see that this process has already begun.

A Change is Gonna Come

The Caveat

This section on the essence of conscious actions and a conscious life—to focus on *We not Me*—must include what some people might see as a caveat. However, it's really just an acknowledgement of one of the criteria for an ethical virtue—the *Doctrine of the Mean*. And the move From *Me to We*, or Conscious Change, is definitely an ethical virtue—the right thing to do.

So let's just take a quick look at the *Doctrine of the Mean*.

The Doctrine of the Mean

Two and a half thousand years ago, Aristotle, the father of virtue ethics, set down a number of criteria for an action to be considered an ethical virtue; one of which was known as *The Doctrine of the Mean*.

And here I don't mean "mean" as in being a mean and nasty, stingy person, but "mean" as the centre point along a continuum.

The *Doctrine of the Mean* is based on a cardinal rule that states: "... right conduct is incompatible with an excess or a deficiency in feelings and actions[3]" It's similar to the fourth truth of Buddhism's Four Noble Truths—the truth of the way leading to suffering's cessation. This is also referred to as the Middle Way, because it avoids the two extremes on either side of it.

So at one end of the *Doctrine of the Mean* continuum is the vice of excess, or overdoing the virtue or the action. And at the other end is the vice of not doing enough of it or not doing it at all.

As an example, when talking about yourself or your actions or achievements, truthfulness is a virtue and sits between the vices of egocentric boasting when done to excess and understating or devaluing yourself when not done sufficiently.

One of the most widely quoted lines of Aristotle's is a good guide that's worth keeping in mind. It goes like this: the mark of virtue is to have feelings, or perform actions, "at the right times, on the right grounds, towards the right people, for the right motive, and in the right way"[4].

This is a version of a very well-known aphorism he had relating to anger. "The person who gets angry at the right things and with the right people, and also in the right way and at the right time and for the right length of time, is commended[5].

A fun example of the *Doctrine of the Mean* can be seen when it comes to laughing. The two vices on either end of the continuum might be raucous laughter at anything, especially at inappropriate times and in inappropriate ways at one end. And never laughing at anything at all, at the other end.

So again in relation to laughing; to paraphrase Aristotle, the mean or the virtue could be described as laughing at the right times, on the right grounds, towards the right people, for the right motive, and in the right way.

The Caveat

Keeping the *Doctrine of the Mean* in mind, let's look at how that applies to the Me-to-We, Conscious concept.

All too often, mothers, and it normally is mothers rather than fathers or even women without a family, spend their lives focusing on just taking care of their family at the expense of their own self-care. This was especially the case before women's empowerment workshops began appearing in recent decades.

For these women it was all about devoting their entire lives to taking care of their family — all about "we". And they never gave themselves any "me" time at all. They were performing the me-to-we virtue to excess and so it was no longer a virtue, but an unethical action, or a vice.

It comes back to the aeroplane analogy and putting on your mask. You've got to put your own mask on first before taking care of your child in the seat beside you.

Similarly, the great many people, many of whom I described in the opening chapter, who just focus on me and not we are demonstrating the vice of a me-to-we deficiency. And going back as far as two and a half thousand years the vice of deficiency has been considered the wrong way to act.

So once again repeating Aristotle aphorism to guide us: Living a conscious life and focusing on *we not me* should be done at the right times, on the right grounds, towards the right people, for the right motive, and in the right way.

Follow those guidelines and you're on your way to becoming a conscious leader of change.

You Can Become a Conscious Leader of Change

With the COVID-19 pandemic at hand, a beautiful story emerged in England about a previously unknown man, World War II veteran Captain Thomas Moore. As he approached his 100th birthday he said, look this pandemic is costing our public health system a fortune—which it is. And the public health system and all those who work in it are doing such a wonderful job—which they are.

So he decided to see if he could raise one thousand pounds, about $1250 US, for the National Health Scheme. His plan was to walk, with the aid of his walking frame, one hundred laps of his garden by his 100th birthday. By the time of his 100th lap, he'd raise nearly thirty-three million pounds, over *$41 million US*.

And so Queen Elizabeth, at the age of a mere 94 and also a World War II veteran, came out of lockdown. Keeping physical-distancing she immediately knighted the 100-year-old champion—Captain, Sir Thomas Moore. Definitely one of the many heart-warming stories to come out of COVID.

Most of the current day articles and books written about Conscious Change have a focus on conscious change in the business arena—conscious capitalism, conscious business, conscious (business) leadership. But as you now know, you can also be a *conscious* (or ethical) leader within your family as my student Chen demonstrated; within your community as the wonderful Captain, Sir Thomas Moore did; or by helping the planet as Greta Thunberg is doing. And even children can be conscious leaders and so role-models in the school yard.

Perhaps you're a massage therapist, or a life coach, an artist, a teacher, a real estate agent, a dog walker, a nurse, a herbalist, someone concerned about climate change, or a parent. No matter what your passion is you can always make a difference to your industry, or to the lives of the people who seek your services, or to your community, or the world at large.

These are indeed very exciting times.

And the Conscious Change Series of Books, beginning here with *Conscious Change Today: From Me to We ...* will introduce you to our current-day world and the many ways you can indeed become a conscious leader of change. And when you do, you'll be adding meaning to your life.

There's nothing more important or more genuinely personally fulfilling and rewarding than to live a meaningful life.

Again, singing is how Johnny Manuel is making a difference. Writing and teaching is how I can make a difference. Walking with the aid of his walking frame leading up to his 100th birthday is how Captain, Sir Thomas Moore did it.

Question ...

So how will you make a difference as a conscious leader of change?

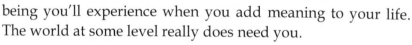

You'll be amazed at the physical, emotional, and overall health and well-being you'll experience when you add meaning to your life. The world at some level really does need you.

The Road Ahead

So what will you find as you journey through the following pages in this first book in the Conscious Change Series.

This book is divided into two parts — Part 1 ~ The Power of Two; and Part 2 ~ Living A Conscious Life Today. Throughout these two parts I continually demonstrate how they're all interrelated.

Everything is Connected to Everything Else

In Part 1 ~ The Power of Two, you'll discover an undeniable global trend based on the quantum theory of global consciousness that parallels the rise in feminine energy, the decline in our traditional patriarchal culture, and an every-growing focus on *conscious* change. This power of two forms the foundation for the conscious changes and the conscious revolution that we're seeing throughout the world today.

Part 2 ~ Living a Conscious Life Today, then examines a number of controversial but interrelated issues including Conscious Feminism; Conscious Masculinity with a blueprint for transforming our patriarchal culture into a culture of total equality for all; COVID-19; and Climate Change.

There's also a chapter addressing the often-asked question, "Has #MeToo Gone Too Far?".

The book concludes with Chapter 22 ~ "Your Call to Action" in which you'll be asked to reflect on your own role in making a difference, today.

Finally, I trust you'll explore the pages ahead with an open mind and an open heart. And as you do, I invite you to continually reflect on the inspirational words of one of the world's greatest philosophers, "The Lorax".

And all that the Lorax left here in this mess
was a small pile of rocks, with one word ... "UNLESS".
Whatever *that* meant, well, I just couldn't guess.

That was long, long ago.
But each day since that day I've sat here and worried and worried away.

Through the years, while my buildings have fallen apart, I've worried about it with all of my heart.

"But *now*," says the Once-ler, Now that *you're* here,

the word of the Lorax seems perfectly clear.

UNLESS *someone like* **YOU**
cares a whole awful lot,
Nothing gets better. No it will not.

~ Dr. Seuss—*The Lorax* ~

The time is now
The choice is yours
It's up to you

~ Part One ~
The
Power of Two

In this, Part One, I introduce you to an undeniable global trend arguably born of the quantum physics theory of Global Consciousness. I pose the question: is this trend behind the irrefutable rise in feminine-energy, and ever-growing focus on *conscious* change? You'll also find plenty of evidence supporting the power of this global trend to bring about these changes.

~ Chapter 3 ~
Patterns & Trends Not Predictions

The key to growth is the introduction of higher levels of consciousness into our awareness.

~ Lao Tzu ~

I used to be like so many people who think things like astrology and numerology are just frivolous fun. And so at a party in the early 1970s, when one of the guests ended up doing free, mini numerology readings for anyone who asked, I put my hand up. It was the first time someone I'd never met before accurately told me the sort of person I was just by looking at my name and date of birth. Words like "amazed" and "impressed" don't come anywhere near describing my reaction.

Nevertheless, again like so many people I went away thinking it was just a fascinating "party-trick" until I began to listen to a professional numerologist, John Arthur Daley, do a weekly spot on radio. Each week I became more and more entranced by what he said to the people phoning in and so I made an appointment to see him for a private, professional reading.

While I was very new to all of that sort of thing, I've always been very open to any insights that might improve my life. A few sessions with John Arthur grew into many years of casual, but ongoing research and a change of name by deed poll to Kashonia Carnegie, after I escaped from a very abusive husband.

The change of name didn't answer the many deep questions I had about how I ended up with that particular type of person for a husband. That would come decades later with even more research, this time into psychological abuse. But numerology remained an "entertaining interest".

And so it should be no surprise that on one occasion in the early 1980s, when procrastination won over the task I was meant to be doing, that I began to reflect on the numbers. This was, of course, long before the Internet and even longer before I had a computer.

But something propelled my thoughts to the years that I'd been living on this planet and what the main events were that I'd seen during those years. Suddenly, a fascinating pattern began to emerge.

The 1950s, with a ten-year emphasis on the number five, the 1960s with a focus on six, and 1970s with the main number being seven, all had a strong emphasis on the numerological characteristics of a five, six, and seven respectively.

Well that got my curious mind really working overtime. Whatever the task was that I was meant to be doing, was no more. I spoke to my elders, and also went to the library and analysed the major global events in the old newspapers back to the 1920s. And the key events in each decade echoed the characteristics of the decade's number.

As an example, five is said to be the number of freedom and change. And the 1950s were the epitome of freedom, renewal, and change after World War II ended the decade before. While six is the number of humanitarianism, love, harmony, truth, justice, and so on; the 1960s saw flower-power, love-ins, and a revolution in social norms, with sit-ins protesting against injustice, and the passing of the world-changing US Civil Rights Act in 1964.

Fascinated by the patterns that emerged when I looked at past decades, I analysed the same patterns moving forward through to 2020 and ended up writing a short paper called "The Power of Two".

The 2 of course relates to our current millennium, the 2000s. And the "power" is all about how that 2 has seemingly empowered women by encouraging the rise of feminine-*energy*, not femininity, but feminine-*energy*, especially that found in those born around the year 2000 and beyond—our Gen Zs.

This was not a "prediction" as much as it was simply stating the trends that the patterns clearly revealed if the same patterns from the past continued on into the future.

The paper was never written for publication. It was just something that I occasionally told people about, and waited to see if the patterns I'd highlighted for future decades would indeed continue to play out, especially after the arrival of the 2000s.

And when they did, I felt that the implications of my findings were far too important to keep quiet any longer.

As a result, the abundance of evidence, insights, and real-world examples that you'll find in the following pages will help you better understand that if the trends continue—and so far they have—there is indeed both a positive and a very exciting side to our current outwardly chaotic world.

In turn, you'll discover the keys to harnessing that 2 power in your personal day-to-day life, ensuring that the potentially peaceful and loving changes in your family life, your work life, and the world beyond are both possible and wonderous.

And globally, if we can all begin to harness that 2 energy, we'll really make a difference to this planet of ours, leading to a more peaceful, loving, understanding, and sustainable world. The sort of world that the average person, when asked, wants to see.

Now it's true that "The Power of Two" is based on what many people consider merely a New Ageist topic like numerology that I too originally thought was just a party-trick. And so a number of people warned me that I'd be foolish, from a scholarly perspective, to make such "nonsense" publicly known. But I deal with those people at the end of the next chapter.

This book is not about presenting hard empirical scientific evidence.

But instead, just like our climate scientists do when telling us about climate change, it's all about offering undeniable, recurring patterns and trends, as is the case with most socio-cultural "scientific" evidence.

And interestingly, as I'll explain shortly, future more recent studies that I undertook demonstrated that not only do the numbers have a specific form of energetic power, but it's the quantum theory of global-consciousness that could well explain how the energetic vibration of numbers can indeed influence world events, such as the rise of feminine-energy with the arrival of the 2000s.

And if we're to harness the power that the 2000s are bringing us, it's essential to have some understanding of the source of that power and how best to use it.

Therefore, in the two chapters that follow you'll find some basic, elementary information so you have a good grounding for what's ahead. And I begin with the elephant in the room. This is regarding the all too often held belief that esoteric subjects are indeed "nonsense". And I do that with a brief discussion on religion, spirituality, and science.

Next, I outline a few fundamentals with regard to energetic vibrations, feminine and masculine *energy*, love-in-action, and the left-brain/right-brain debate, all of which are relevant to the power of two. That will allow you to easily reflect back on those definitions and explanations when I demonstrate how surprisingly accurate my forecasts were back in the 1980s, all based on the numerical patterns I was seeing.

As you'll discover there's never been a time when cosmic energy has been more supportive of us all working together to create a new world of peace, love, and sustainability.

Heads-Up

Finally, just a heads-up about the importance of repetition.

Has this ever happened to you?

 You've just read a page or two of a non-fiction book and suddenly you realise that you can't remember what you just read. It's quite a common occurrence. But if someone asked you a specific question about the page you read, you'd probably remember. And that's why one of the keys to learning and growth is repetition, or review.

Amusingly, one of the Amazon comments for a really powerful book I once bought said: "The author has the annoying habit of restating his main thesis *ad nausem* as if this makes his case more true (Spoiler alert: it doesn't)" [emphasis and "spoiler alert" in the original text].

So let me warn you up front. If the same person reads this book he'll probably, ignorantly, say the same thing.

What the person making that comment failed to understand is that, like me, the author was not wanting to "make his case more true" by repeating concepts. But instead he was doing a number of very important things.

The main ones being that he was reminding the reader of the importance of what was being repeated, in case it had slipped past them. It's often said that we need to read something at least six times before it's really seen and understood.

And also the repetition is a form of review, something I can do at a live event, but not in a book.

As I used to say to my MBA students, if you ever hear me repeating something please make an extra note of whatever it was because you'll probably get a question on that in the end of semester examinations.

So in the pages ahead, when I do repeat something or refer back to something I've said before, it's not because I'm old and have forgotten what I've previously spoken about. It's because review or *repetition is one of the mothers of skill and learning*.

I talk about this and other keys to learning and growth in my *Essential Guide for Conscious Leaders of Change ~ Keys to Learning and Growth* available on Amazon, early 2021.

~ Chapter 4 ~
Religion, Spirituality, & Science

*It's clearly evident that most events of a widespread
nature draw their causes from the enveloping heavens.*
~ Claudius Ptolemy ~
(100-168 CE)

I f you're reading this book, then chances are that you're at least open to topics such as numerology and astrology and perhaps a whole range of other so-called paranormal events such as remote viewing, clairvoyance, out of body experiences, near death experiences, and general telepathic communication, to name but a few. And so you're probably interested in finding out more.

Or you could just be a beautiful open-minded, life-long learner who is open to all things in this amazing universe of ours, and so be very wise as well as beautiful.

As you've no doubt already experienced, there are many people who are totally closed to new ideas of any kind, let alone so-called flaky ideas such as astrology and numerology.

And if someone holds a firm belief in something, no matter what it is, logic and rational argument will rarely change that belief. It normally takes some sort of deep emotional experience before a change will occur. So in this chapter I'm not expecting mind-changing miracles, because I don't intend to use any deep manipulative emotional arguments.

Instead, I just intend to present a number of, what I hope are, thought-provoking ideas and questions. And if you belong to the closed-minded brigade maybe you'll at least give the questions some thought.

If on the other hand you're one of the open-minded readers, then you might find some of these ideas and questions of use when speaking with others not as wise as you are.

The first and most obvious question of all to ask a numerology/astrology skeptic is; on what do you base that belief? What is your evidence for thinking that way?

Generally, the two main arguments are (1) the God argument: "Oh I believe in God!" Or "Oh no, I'm religious". I've often encountered both of those on many occasions. And (2) the scientific argument — there's no scientific evidence that paranormal things like numerology can do what they say it does.

And really there is some overlap in both the God argument and the scientific argument.

So let's have a quick look at them both.

The Birth of Religious Beliefs

Religious beliefs in one form or another have been around for millennia and over that time have evolved in many different ways.

Going back to ancient times, amazing things happened that could not be explained by the physical world as it was understood in those days. And so as the human mind likes to make sense of things, the only way that the people of the day could explain what happened was to say that it must have been God, or the gods, that were responsible.

Goodness even today, many insurance policies will not cover "Acts of God" – such as storms and flooding. Forget about the many possible science-based human causes for that flooding.

And when something is constantly repeated and believed generation after generation after generation, it becomes so entrenched in the human psyche that the only question is does the particular belief wear a Christian colour, or an Islamic colour, the colour of an Eastern tradition, or the colour of one of the other estimated four thousand plus religious faiths[6]?

However, a far more interesting question arises if we consider another very ancient form of belief. While many billions of people around the world still firmly believe in "God" in some form today; in our 21st century a far smaller percentage firmly believe in more esoteric subjects like astrology or the ancient study of numbers and their meanings. And even talk of "harmonic vibrations", which are based on science, is enough to have people put up an impervious "rubbish" shield.

So why has the study of numbers and astrology as an example, been so ridiculed by so many when God is just as intangible?

Science and Religion

It's often erroneously said that there's no connection between science and religion. And that might have been a legitimate belief in centuries past. But today certain areas of science, such as quantum theory, mirrors many religious beliefs exactly. Today, quantum physics can explain what the ancients could not explain and so attributed to God, or the gods.

In the early 2000s, as a spiritual agnostic I started studying quantum physics in a bid to answer my long-held question about the unknown higher power I felt existed. And yes, I discovered that God is alive and well and its name is "quantum physics". Even so-called miracles can be explained by quantum physics, especially regarding local and nonlocal events.

One of the things I love about quantum physics is the claim made by most quantum physicists that anyone who says they have a good understanding of quantum physics clearly doesn't understand it at all. That makes me feel a lot more confident about what I've always considered was my very elementary understanding of the field.

And if you're totally new to quantum physics/quantum theory, I recommend you begin by watching the 2004 docu-drama *What the Bleep Do We (K)now!?*. It runs for 1.49 hours. And in 2006 an extended 2 ½ hour version was released called *What the Bleep!?: Down the Rabbit Hole*, which contains additional interviews and extended versions of some of the original interviews.

Now I acknowledge that *What the Bleep* was criticised for some questionable inaccuracies due to its bias in attempting to get a specific message across. But you're not watching it to get a university degree in quantum physics. And because of the way it's produced, it's very easy to watch and understand, especially if you watch it with an open-mind.

Then after watching the movie, read the little book *Beyond the Bleep: the definitive unauthorized guide to What the Bleep*. It's a little 288-page, pocket-sized book written by Alexandra Bruce. It has no connection whatsoever with the movie, and so pulls apart some of the alleged inaccuracies and biases in the film.

After that, these new perspectives on the paranormal and consciousness will seem a lot more legitimate.

Yet why are so many very religious people so closed to the notion that God is definitely alive and well, but it just goes by the name of Quantum Physics?

That's certainly a discussion for another day.

Astrology—"a way to look at the world"

There's a definite movement today towards the paranormal by Millennials and Gen X. As one young person said "We take astrology very seriously, but we also don't necessarily believe in it completely. It's just a way to look at the world[7]."

And whenever I talk about astrology, I'm not talking about the non-specific few lines churned-out in weekly magazines. They have virtually no link to reality and are partly responsible for giving the field its bad reputation.

I'm talking about the sort of personal astrological analyses put together by a professional astrologer who's spent countless years learning their craft.

Many years ago, when I was "between jobs" I decided to begin a formal 3-year certificate course in astrology. Sadly, I only completed about six months study before my new job meant that I just didn't have the time to devote to my astrological studies.

But it was as a result of the assignments that I had to complete during that brief six-month period that I became a total convert. Yes, a convert to the amazing insights that are available when a professional astrological analysis is done—all based on aspects of cosmic energy in one form or another.

We've all heard the wild stories from people who have to deal with the public on the nights of a full moon. And I was one of them.

As a night-time talk-back radio broadcaster I always prepared myself for some *very* strange calls on the night of a full moon. And my preparations were never in vain. Yet scientists insist that there is nothing in that full-moon weirdness at all.

But they are probably scientists who've never had to work with the public on the night of a full moon.

And even rational arguments that are often put forward are rejected. For instance, if the moon affects tides, and sea creatures, why wouldn't the moon, the stars, and other astral bodies also affect humans in some way?

After all, astrophysicist, Neil deGrasse Tyson, explains:

The atoms of our bodies are traceable to stars that manufactured them in their cores and exploded these enriched ingredients across our galaxy, billions of years ago. For this reason, we are biologically connected to every other living thing in the world. We are chemically connected to all molecules on Earth. And we are atomically connected to all atoms in the universe. We are not figuratively, but literally stardust.

Arguments like those should be enough for the average thinking person to say, well I don't quite understand how it works in practice, but in the words of the MythBusters, I guess it's certainly *plausible*.

It's like me and live television, or any television for that matter. I just cannot get my mind around the fact that pictures can fly though the atmosphere and land in my TV set. But they do.

I constantly hear of stories like this next one that I read recently.

A social cognitive scientist said:

Let me state first that I consider astrology a cultural or psychological phenomenon, not a scientific one. Full-fledged astrology provides a powerful vocabulary to capture not only personality and temperament, but also life's challenges and opportunities. To the extent that one simply learns this vocabulary, it may be appealing as a rich way of representing (not explaining or predicting) human experiences and life events, and identifying some possible paths of coping[8].

To me that sounds like a scientist who fully believes that there is certainly something to astrology, but they are also covering their academic butt.

Science is a wonderfully amazing field — I love it. After all, I hold a Master of Science degree, myself. But I would never reject as "nonsense" anything, just because it can't be explained by the Scientific Experiment or Reductive Materialism.

Sadly there are some areas of science where challenging dogmatic assumptions is just "not permitted", no matter how much scientific testing has demonstrated that those dogmatic assumptions are at best questionable. We live in a wonderous and mysterious universe where arguably even out-dated hard and fast laws *should* be questioned.

Hungarian-born philosopher of science, systems theorist, and advocate of quantum consciousness, Ervin Laszlo[9], discusses a range of so-called "paranormal" events in his 2017 paper "Consciousness Is Mind Beyond Space and Time: The New Paradigm". Yet there was a time when paranormal events such as remote viewing, clairvoyance, out of body experiences, and the like were also considered merely hot air and just a thing for getting money out of a gullible person.

Now sure, there'll always be cases of charlatans at work in these areas. But these days there's also an abundance of repeated scientific experiments documenting legitimate events in all of these fields.

And so in more recent years, it's quantum physics that's added a whole new dimension to our understanding of our mysterious world and also the so-called paranormal, including astrology.

After all, just consider neutrinos. Neutrinos are sub-atomic particles that come from several different cosmic sources. And every second of every day and every night, literally trillions of neutrinos pass through every human body, including yours and mine. If nothing else, is it not at least plausible that these connect us to the stars in some way as Neil deGrasse Tyson suggested? And is it not therefore possible that something like that can link us to some form of astrological energy?

In classical physical and traditional science, the scientist wants to be able to objectively see the various stages of the experiments they're conducting. By contrast, in quantum physics the process is not objective and it's not visible. The only thing that can be recorded is the *outcome* — a bit like astrology and numerology.

So the "more traditional" scientists still strongly argue that quantum physics is definitely not a science, but just an idle philosophy.

Closed-minded, egocentric, disciplinary chauvinism at its best, or should that be at its worst.

The Italian theoretical physicist, Carlo Rovelli[10], who's often referred to as the new Stephen Hawking, said that we need to be open to different ways of understanding our world. He continued: "If you look at the scientists of the past, even the greats like Einstein, Heisenberg, or Newton, none of them had this arrogance of thinking that *they* had the only access to understanding."

And it's that sort of closed-minded "arrogance" that Rovelli spoke of that has led us to our current environmental crises.

But even if you remain skeptical about astrological influences on our lives, when it comes to basic numerology in the fundamental way I'll be referring to it, there's nothing to be skeptical about at all. Its origin is just basic logic.

Numerology? It's Just Basic Common Sense

The whole theory of "the power of two" is based on what many people consider the New Age nonsense of numerology — the study of numbers. But far from the study of numbers coming out of the New Age movement of the 1970s; attributing certain characteristics to numbers is just basic logic that goes back thousands and thousands of years.

Now I don't want to turn this into a numerology text book; there are plenty of those available already. At this stage I just want to highlight the source of the logical characteristics for the two numbers that are primarily featured in this book — the numbers 1 and 2. And I'll also add a few words about number 3 to show the progression.

Let's start with the number 1. And I'll make this extremely simplistic because often the more intelligent the person, the more they attempt to think at unnecessary higher levels, and so the more simplistic the example needs to be.

Take 1 single apple and imagine it on the table in front of you. There it is — big, red, and shiny. It's standing on its own, alone, *independently*. And because it's there on its own it is *superior* to, and in *control* of, the nothing else that's there with it. So definitely a *Me* focus because it's all there is.

Therefore you might say that the characteristics of apple #1, or just plain number 1, include independence, superiority, control and a *Me* focus.

Now imagine that a second apple suddenly appears and you have two bright shiny apples in front of you. The second apple, apple number 2, is now a *partner* to apple #1. And if apple #2 had conscious thought it might think well I'm the newcomer so I will be *subservient* to apple #1 because apple #1 has been here longer and knows more about what's going on in the world. And so I will *cooperate* with #1. Clearly a **We** focus.

And by the way, there is an argument that apples do have a form of conscious thought but that's also a discussion for another day.

So the characteristics of apple #2, or just plain number 2, are things like partnership, cooperation, and a **We** focus.

Now let's move those thoughts onto humans instead of apples.

You have one single, independent human. And from an evolutionary, patriarchal perspective, and certainly from a Biblical perspective, that first single human to arrive is a man. So just like the apple, he'll have the characteristics of the 1 — independence, superiority, control, and a **Me** focus. And in Chapter 17, on Conscious Masculinity, I talk about the positive evolutionary need for men to be considered superior, all of which has now changed in our 21st century world.

What happens next? Eve arrives — the second human. And like the second apple she realises that to survive she needs to *cooperate* and promote the *partnership* she has with human number one. And this will include making the *peace* when necessary, using *tact, diplomacy, consultation*, and so a **We** *attitude.*

And again, some of the characteristics of the number 2 in numerology include, yes, partnership and cooperation, and also peace, tact, diplomacy, consultation, **We not Me**, *et cetera.*

Then a third human is there. And a major characteristic of the number 3 is creativity. And there are so many examples to demonstrate that three people working on a problem will be much more creative than two, and definitely more than one person on their own.

And on it goes from there.

So back thousands of years, the study of numbers was not *woo woo* esoteric stuff. Believing in a mysterious God was a lot more *woo wooish* and esoteric. The study of numbers was just the basic logical recognition of the obvious characteristics of one versus two, versus, three, versus four ... people living in our world of relationships. The recognition of the characteristics of one person on their own, then the changes when the second person arrives, and even more changes when the third, and then the fourth, and fifth person arrives, and so on.

So in essence, numerology is just about the study of numbers and giving different numbers different obvious associated characteristics. And it's been with us for millennia.

In the next chapter I'll explain in a little more depth the characteristics of male-energy that's obviously related to the number 1 versus the characteristics of female-energy that's obviously associated with the number 2.

And what is it that brings those characteristics to life in our world? I suggest that it's all about the quantum theory of *global consciousness*[11].

Global Consciousness

If you're new to global consciousness, sometimes called field consciousness, here's a brief explanation of what it's all about, complete with some familiar down-to-earth examples. This will explain the veracity of the power of two in our new 2000 millennium.

Again in classical physics, the reference to "fields" is all about physical things such as gravitational fields and electromagnetic fields. But in quantum physics these fields of consciousness have no exchange of physical energy across space and time, nor a time/space location. And so field or global consciousness experiments are actually a demonstration of the reality of what is generally known as a nonlocal event.

Hang in there, it gets easier from here.

Some of these experiments have been conducted using small groups of people engaged in personal development workshops through to millions and even billions of people world-wide, all with fascinating results.

Many experiments take the form of testing changes in the readings from equipment placed in various locations throughout the world when major events take place, such as the handing down of the O.J. Simpson verdict, the playing of the Super Bowl, and the death and funeral of Diana, the Princess of Wales.

Regardless of the size or importance of the event, the key is that the event is noteworthy enough to hold the full attention of the participants being studied. The idea is to see if there's a significant change in the instrument's readings when the emotions of groups of individuals are focused on the same single event.

And researchers have found that when a group's consciousness is fully focused on the same event, a difference definitely occurs compared to the times when their focus is scattered. While these differences are not always significant, the differences are consistent from one study to the next, and that *is* significant.

This indicates that our thoughts and emotions can, and indeed do, influence the planet and all those dwelling here. Surely that's something pretty wild to consider.

Dean Radin[12] talks about a very simple study that's been done monitoring the weather on both commencement and graduation days at Princeton University.

Now everyone wants a fine day because many events are held in the open. So naturally everyone involved automatically and non-consciously focuses on having a fine day. And while it might be raining in nearby towns, it's almost always fine at Princeton during those events. One year, even though the overall day at Princeton was extremely wet, the couple of hours during the ceremony itself were fine.

And that always reminds me of something that happened to me many years ago. And seeing as, to the best of my knowledge, I was the only person involved, maybe it was purely "coincidental". Who knows.

I was living in Far North Queensland, in the tropical region of Australia, and I had what was for me at the time a very important audition at the local television station. Unfortunately, the audition was on the same day as my car had to go to the garage for some work and so I had to walk to the TV studio. And that was okay because it was only about a kilometre from home.

But a couple of hours before the appointment the heavens opened and the rain flooded down. After all the normal comments to myself of "oh no"; "what am I going to do", "I'll end up at the TV studio looking like a drowned rat'. I made a decision.

I decided to immediately get dressed and ready to walk out the door, with at least one hour+ to spare. Which I did.

Then during that last hour I just sat quietly and focused non-stop, as hard as I could, on the most beautiful brilliant sunshine and a bright blue sky, and having it remain that way until I arrived at the TV studio.

With just a couple of minutes to go, the rain was still bucketing-down.

But not to be deterred, I continued to focus on brilliant sunshine and a bright blue sky.

Then, and I kid you not, the moment the clock ticked over to the time I had to leave, the most beautiful bright rain-free sunshine appeared. With eyes the size of saucers I grabbed an umbrella, just in case I needed it to get back home and off I went.

I stepped onto the covered veranda of the studio with the sun still shining. I walked up to the front door. The moment I began to open the front door, the heavens opened again. But hey, I was there, dry, and looking like a million dollars as I had also envisioned.

And yes, I certainly needed the umbrella to get home because the rain continued well into that night. And yes, I did look like a drowned rat when I got home.

Now even those at The Global Consciousness Project might well say that that event was purely a coincidence. And one day I will ask them. But it is certainly a true story that I'll always remember.

So it's this field/global consciousness that offers a plausible explanation of how the number two, in the 2000s, can indeed influence our current rise of feminine-energy. And before giving you numerous real-life examples through-out the book, in the next chapter I'll briefly explain what feminine-energy is all about.

Even though different peoples in different cultures might not use the traditional Western calendar on a personal level, in interacting on a global level the Western calendar must come to the fore in one way or another.

So here we have almost eight billion people focusing year in and year out on the single most significant and constant number on a calendar. And since the arrival of our new millennium, that's the number two. And that's definitely the largest and most consistent on-going sample size ever for a global consciousness experiment.

So how can our current world not be influenced by the characteristics that are in harmony with the vibrations of the number two? All very exciting indeed! Or at the very least, thought-provoking, don't you think?

The other thing to keep in mind is that people don't begin to focus on a new year, or a new decade, let alone a new millennium, on January 1st. That's why the influence of a new decade number begins prior to the new decade itself. This is especially the case with something as big as our new millennium.

People world-wide began focusing on the 2000s many years before. And so the influence of the number two began to appear in the 1990s and continued to strengthen the closer we got to the 2000s.

As you reflect on the power of two and journey through the following pages, I invite you to keep this notion of global consciousness in mind, especially with regard to its potential contribution to any change-the-world strategy, or personal life-changes you might be considering.

Just take a moment to imagine the incredible power millions and millions of positive like-minded people world-wide would have if they all focused on the same thing—living a peaceful, loving, ethical, and sustainable life, all of which are characteristics of the number 2, as I'll explain shortly.

Yet sadly, all too many people just focus on the negatives, both in their own personal world and the world overall.

Today, that cosmic-quantum-energy is supporting that loving and sustainable life in the metaphysical world. But it's up to each and every one of us to bring it to life in our physical world.

If you want to explore this topic a little further, you can find my *Conscious Leader's Guide for ~ What is Consciousness*, on Amazon early 2021.

A Final Reflection

A bit like beliefs in climate change — at this point you are either open to the possibility of cosmic energy impacting our world, related to the two of the 2000s, or you're not. And as I discuss towards the end of this book, again like climate change there can be dramatic positive and negative consequences to having an open-mind, or a closed-mind to the whole thing, both personally and also globally.

Finally, if anyone tries to tell you that astrology or numerology has no foundation because it makes no sense, remind them of the erroneous ridicule that Einstein received.

Afterall, Einstein and those who continued to follow-on told us that space is curved by matter; and that parallel lines always cross; and that light comes as little packets of energy that we now call photons; oh and reality isn't really real, it's fuzzy. How wild can you get!

And yet there are those who condemn numerology because *it* doesn't make sense! As I said before, we live in a wonderous and *mysterious* world.

Nobel Prize winning Quantum Physicist, Richard Feynman, described it like this. The rules of quantum physics are so strange and so "screwy" that you can't believe them. But they are indeed reality and we all have to get used to it.

As a result, physicists and chemists have been using these weird rules for decades to invent transistors, computers, lasers, nuclear reactors, cameras, mobile/cell phones, MRI scanners, solar panels, medicines, and so much more.

So, if someone unreservedly ridicules something like numerology or astrology without at least a budding depth of understanding, all they're doing is embarrassing themselves with their display of both arrogance and ignorance.

Remember that understanding the physics of our world allows us to make better, more informed decisions, which is one reason why a multi-perspective view of the world is a significant key to wisdom.

~ Chapter 5 ~
What is Feminine-*Energy*?

The atoms of our bodies are traceable to stars that manufactured them in their cores and exploded these enriched ingredients across our galaxy, billions of years ago. For this reason, we are biologically connected to every other living thing in the world. We are chemically connected to all molecules on Earth. And we are atomically connected to all atoms in the universe. We are not figuratively, but literally stardust.

~ Neil deGrasse Tyson ~

Let's now begin with a brief explanation of what feminine-*energy* is all about, starting with the "energy" part of feminine-energy, because it underpins the global changes we're currently seeing and also the way to a beautiful future.

Cosmic or Spiritual *Energy*

Now if the idea of cosmic or spiritual energy sounds a bit WOO-WOOish, take heart because you're just one of many people who erroneously think that way.

But in this very short section, let me give you an introduction to cosmic energy. However, if you find your eyes beginning to glaze-over, just let your non-conscious continue for the remaining paragraph or two.

Okay, so everything on the planet works due to a form of harmonic electrical energy—our thought patterns, our brain, our body, the plants, the weather, the works. Much of this electrical energy can also be referred to as harmonic vibrations, or frequencies, or resonances.

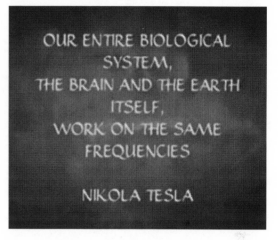

OUR ENTIRE BIOLOGICAL SYSTEM,
THE BRAIN AND THE EARTH ITSELF,
WORK ON THE SAME FREQUENCIES

NIKOLA TESLA

One of many fascinating examples of how the Earth's "energy" or harmonic vibrations affects us all comes from solid scientific research conducted by the HeartMath Institute's Global Coherence Initiative.[13]

This research shows that the actual electrical frequencies, or energies, in our brain are influenced by the global electromagnetic frequencies known as the Schumann Resonances that are "beamed down" from the cosmos. And the natural coherent rhythm of our heart is in harmony with the Field-Line Resonances that are affected by the solar winds that, again, are beamed-down from space.

So those who are convinced that "cosmic energy" and "harmonic vibrations" are just New Age waffle, are again just showing their closed-minded ignorance.

Now on to the feminine and masculine parts of feminine-*energy* and masculine-*energy*.

Feminine-<u>*Energy*</u> versus Masculine-<u>*Energy*</u>

Feminine-energy and masculine-energy is sometimes referred to as masculine and feminine cosmic energy or spiritual energy. And in talking about masculine-*energy* and feminine-*energy* it's important to stress that I'm not talking about one form of energy being good and the other bad. Nor am I talking about female and male, nor women and men. I'm talking about attitudes, actions, and mind-sets that are most commonly found in either men or women. In other words, ways of thinking and acting in our world.

It's true that women are more likely to have stronger feminine-energy and men stronger masculine-energy. But many heterosexual men have strong feminine-*energy*, just as many heterosexual women exude masculine-*energy*.

One well known example is the first female Prime Minister of the United Kingdom (1979-1990), Margaret Thatcher, who was known as the Iron-Lady because of her very masculine-*energy*. And although I can't compete with Margaret Thatcher, nor would I want to, but because of the way I was brought up as a child who was meant to be a boy, I too generally convey a strong masculine-energy. Although I can occasionally have my feminine moments as well.

Yet in the past men were taught to suppress their feminine-energy, especially their emotions, just as women were taught to suppress their masculine-energy and just be submissive. But as you're probably aware, that's all changing.

Meanwhile, it's essential to note the generally accepted characteristics of masculine-energy versus feminine-energy in case you're not familiar with those traits. This will be very important in future chapters.

Characteristics of Masculine-Energy

Masculine-energy is commonly known for domination, control, power-over, independence, impatience, aggression, individuality, and self-centred ambition. As I'm sure you'd agree, these all have a *me* focus.

Interestingly, today in the field of virtue ethics, these are all considered vices, which of course are always considered negative. Yet anthropology and evolutionary biology explains that those so-called negative-masculine traits had a very important evolutionary role to play in prehistoric times, something I touch on a little more in Chapter 17 — Conscious Masculinity.

But masculine-energy is also known for traits that these days are considered positive like analytical, concrete, left-brain thinking, logic, reason, and mathematics. Symbolically, masculine-energy is also associated with the sun, the number one, straight lines, and sharp corners.

Characteristics of Feminine-Energy

By contrast, for millennia positive feminine-energy is all about a *we* focus. It's known for moral virtues including partnerships, love consciousness, peacemaking, power-with, co-operation, tact, agreement, consultation, intuition, the abstract, patience, nurturing, creativity, diplomacy, and consideration, as well as music, imagination, wholistic right-brain thinking, and a wholistic spiritual view of the world. And symbolically, feminine-energy is associated with the number two, the moon, water, circles, curves, and swirls.

The image on the cover of this book is a perfect representation of our rising feminine-energy — the depiction of the rising full moon over the water. So too are the curves and swirls on the title and author fonts on the cover.

The whole power of two associated with our new 2000-millennium, and the rise in the status of women can be summed up in the following figure.

> ✓ **The number 2 is the symbolic number associated with women and feminine-energy**
>
> ✓ **Positive Feminine-Energy Traits are the same as Moral Virtues**
>
> ✓ **Therefore, the number 2, and so our new 2000-millennium, has the same symbolic characteristics as Moral Virtues**
>
> ✓ **It's these same Moral Virtues that form the foundation of *Conscious* activities and the move from *Me* to *We***

Now just as masculine-energy can display some positive traits, feminine-energy can also express some negative characteristics such as jealousy, gossiping, being superficial, self-centredness, whining, lack of consideration, manipulation, being a gold digger, vengefulness, and snobbishness.

So while masculine-energy and feminine-energy can both have positive and negative traits, it's up to us here on Earth to use our conscious awareness of these energies to ensure that the positive reigns supreme.

dominant, and creatives were right-brain dominant. And so for many decades now the left-brain versus right-brain descriptors have been in common use. Many books and courses featuring these descriptors have been published such as *The Right-Brain Manager*, and *Drawing on the Right Side of the Brain*, and so forth.

However some little while back, with the increase in technology that can measure the activity in the brain, this left-brain/right-brain distinction was totally discredited.

First, people were getting their knickers in a knot saying "Oh but we don't have two brains—a left-brain and a right-brain. We only have a single brain that has two hemispheres."

And yes that's true, but still the terms left-brain and right brain are what's commonly used.

Then it was argued that no matter what we do, both sides of our brain are activated to some degree and so there was no basis for distinguishing left-brain versus right-brain activities. And that's also very true, but only in part.

It's at this point that I'd love to go into pages of philosophical analysis as to why studies discrediting the commonly accepted left-brain/right-brain theories are far too much of a generalisation with far too many holes. But you'll be relieved to hear, that I won't do that.

Instead I'll just make this very basic and simple and say that relatively recent studies, especially those by Dr. Iain McGilchrist,[14] have honed the left-brain/right-brain distinctions in a very interesting way.

Dr. McGilchrist suggests that by rigidly saying the left-brain does this and the right-brain does that, we're approaching the topic from the wrong perspective. Instead of asking what each hemisphere *does*, we should be asking *how* each hemisphere does what it does. This then gives us some subtle differences to the original theories.

In keeping with those who want to debunk the left-brain/right-brain distinctions; yes, it's true that we use both hemispheres simultaneously when we do various things. But reflecting back on a far more refined view of the original idea is that the two hemispheres are approaching the same activity simultaneously, *yet from totally different perspectives.* And we don't consciously realise that these two things are going on in our brain at the same time.

The left-hemisphere approaches the task from a narrow, linear, cause and effect perspective where we must follow the rules, and things are fixed, certain, and result from mechanically putting bits and pieces together, 1,2,3. This is definitely masculine-energy in action.

By contrast, the right-brain sees things wholistically, from a quantum perspective of massive, complex, interconnected systems, which is feminine-energy in action. This right-brain perspective gives us a much deeper and richer view of the world.

Even with these new ideas on how the two hemispheres do things simultaneously, the original reason, logic, mathematics left-brain view and the creative, artistic, right-brain view are still valid.

I'll leave it at that at this stage. However, having acknowledged the right-*hemisphere*/left-*hemisphere* debate, because of common usage, I'll continue to use the original metaphoric left-brain/right-brain terms when required.

Now it's time to move from background *information* on to *knowledge* and maybe even on to *wisdom* and our new world.

~ Chapter 6 ~
Is It the Two or Not the Two ~ That is the Question

Wisdom is saying: My mind is open.
Wherever I am, I'm just beginning.

~ Leo Buscaglia ~

As you'll recall, the original "Power of Two" paper that I wrote in the mid-1980s was based on the recurring patterns that I saw after comparing the previous decades with the characteristics of the main decade-numbers in each of those decades. These are characteristics that have been around for millennia.

Based on the same numerical correlations, I then mapped out what the decades, through to the 2020s might hold in store if the same number correlations continued into the future as they had in the past.

As I did this, my focus was on the exciting energetic influence the number two might have on us all once we reached the 2000s. And so far, coincidence or not, those trends have played out exactly as the numbers indicated they would.

In Appendix A, I've listed the decades from the 1920s to the 1990s, in which I've highlighted some of these fascinating decade-number-characteristic parallels.

And even if you're still at all dubious about the notion that numbers could influence events, I do so hope you'll at least check out the appendix. And when you do, you'll see that the broad correlations between the events in each of those eight decades and the key number associated with each are undeniable. Surely the correlations are far too consistent to be purely coincidental.

Now it is true that during those decades many things happened that had nothing to do with the specific number-decade characteristics. And sure I'm well aware of the aphorism "correlation does not imply causation". And so I'm just talking about the overall major *trends* for each decade.

Like Twitter, even though you're constantly told what's "trending", there are also thousands of other topics being discussed.

So whether or not you believe in the influence of the numbers is up to you, but the evidence of the rise in what the number two represents is patently clear — wholistic, creative, right-brain, feminine-energy, and all that that entails, as explained in Chapter 5. In other words, "conscious" characteristics.

And so here we are, now in the third decade of the 2000s. Again, could it really be just a coincidence that this major increase in feminine-energy is indeed happening throughout the world at this time? Well, I don't know about you, but I've never believed in "coincidences".

Call the events that have been taking place since the mid-1990s trends, or patterns, or something similar. But please, do not just dismiss them as mere coincidences. Whatever the cause, these patterns of events, or trends if you prefer, have been recurring without missing a beat for far too long to be merely a coincidence.

Even so, I acknowledge that for many people the talk about the rise of cosmic feminine-energy and conscious change based on the number two will be a leap too far; far too far. And if that's the case for you, that's fine. All I ask is that you don't let those limiting views block your open-mind to the potential *opportunities* open to us all at this time.

Instead, look at the evidence that I've presented including the quantum theory of global consciousness, as well as what's ahead, all with an open-mind.

Nevertheless, if that's still not you, just turn to your nightly TV news for evidence of this rise in the status of women alone. So too, the ever-increasing focus on our current unethical systems and activities that are characteristic of many aspects of so-called negative masculine-energy. As I'll demonstrate in the coming chapters, these negative activities are in decline, or at least being questioned.

Therefore, if you can't categorically disprove the influence of the number 2, due to the new 2000 millennium, then surely as the physicist, Carlo Rovelli, suggested it would be sheer arrogance not to at least admit that it's *plausible.*

Martin Luther King, Jr. put it this way: "Nothing in all the world is more dangerous than sincere ignorance and conscientious stupidity". Again, look at where we are today with our climate change crises.

Other Ways to Look at the Changes

Setting aside the effects of COVID-19 that I'll come to in Chapter 19, undeniable evidence abounds that the world is experiencing a major change and you can interpret the reason behind those changes at this time in whatever way is most comfortable for you.

Who can really say for sure where these changes have come from. And it's really not important to know for sure. It's certainly not important to me to be right about the numbers, or the cosmic energy, or anything else for that matter.

What I am attached to is the old *Carpe Diem* — seize the day, or certainly seize the opportunity that's currently knocking on our door. An opportunity to add great meaning to our world and your life by making a major difference somewhere, somehow, in this world of ours.

And when an opportunity comes knocking, even if it's only a gentle tap, we must *take action.* Or in the words of Anthony Robbins: "Take *Massive* Action". Oprah said once: "God [the universe] always whispers first". If we don't take any notice of the whisper the message will get stronger, and louder, and tougher, and more painful, until we finally take action.

The universe has been whispering since the 1990s and it's now reaching a crescendo and all of our visionary and spiritual leaders agree. Indeed could the coronavirus be the stronger, and louder, and tougher, and certainly more painful message we've all been sent because it's taken us too long to take action? Maybe? Maybe not? I really have no idea, but it is, at least, worth a thought.

Between 2009 and 2011, I conducted over sixty webinar/teleseminar interviews with some of the world's leading spiritual thinkers and visionaries in fields as diverse as human potential, cosmology, physics, storytelling, education, sustainability, laughter, sustainable town planning, psychology, marketing from the heart, love, horticultural botany, climate change, the crop circle phenomena,

Egyptology, community development, leadership, sociology, body-mind-spirit science, to name but a few.

My guests included names such as Dr. Jean Houston, Dr. Anodea Judith, Dr. Riane Eisler, Dr. David Loye, Arjuna Ardagh, Dr. Genie Laborde, Christine Kloser, Dr. Judith Sherven & Dr. Jim Sniechowski, HeartMath's Sheva Carr, Dr. Wendy Sarkissian, Dr. Carl Calleman, Lucy Pringle, Dr. Paul LaViolette, Dr. David Gershon, Dr. Joel Goodman, and the list goes on. And without exception, the research and work of each and every one of these beautiful and highly intelligent leaders clearly demonstrated that this is indeed a time of massive change.

There can be dozens of ways to reach the same destination and only an anachronistic or closed-mind would say that there is only one way. And so these interviews were a great example of unity in diversity as they all presented different reasons for their predicted global change, supported by different evidence, based on their personal fields of expertise.

And just because they all have different perspectives; it doesn't mean that any of them have to be wrong so that others can be right. It's just a beautiful example of our multi-perspective world—a unity of outcomes from a very diverse range of visionaries and their diverse disciplines.

As an example, I base a time of massive change on the 2 energy and the associated rise of positive feminine-energy—Conscious Change. While Dr. Anodea Judith examines a chakra model to demonstrate that we've left a time when the "love of power" was supreme and have entered the time of realising the "power of love". Interestingly, the "love of power" is a clear example of negative masculine-energy versus the "power of love" which is positive feminine-energy and *conscious* change at work.

Author, psychologist, and co-founder of the human potential movement, Dr. Jean Houston calls this time on our planet, *Jump Time*. In her book of the same name she says:

> Jump Time is a whole system transition, a condition of interactive change that affects every aspect of life as we know it. It is the changing of the guard on every level, in which every "given" is quite literally up for grabs. It is the momentum behind the drama of the world, the breakdown and breakthrough of every old way of being, knowing, relating, governing, and believing. It shakes the foundations of all and everything. And it allows for another order of reality to come into time.

Meanwhile, scientist and New York Times best-selling author, Gregg Braden, refers to this time in much the same way as Jean Houston talks about "Jump Time".

Gregg Braden calls this time the *New World Age,* which he describes as the beginning of a major transition. For him, this transition is based on "sweeping away" the failures, pain, suffering, judgments, and biases of the past and "embracing the best of what we've learned" and growing from there.

This is suggestive of the relatively new field of Appreciative Inquiry[15] which is a positive change process that builds on the things that are currently working and dismisses problems that aren't working, as opposed to merely trying to solve the existing problems.

What that means is if there is indeed some form of cosmic or universal energy supporting and promoting major change at this time, we need to "seize the day" and build on that positive energy by working together to create a genuinely loving or "conscious" world.

And if you'd like to receive a free copy of several of these particularly inspirational and timeless interviews, just fill in the form on https://www.ConsciousChangeToday.com/subscribe/

They're all the same thing

Whether we talk about the power of the number 2 that's changing the world due to the global focus on the 2000s by Global Consciousness, or just the adoption of positive feminine-energy; or the development of a right-brain bias; or the cultivation of ethics-in-action; or love-in-action; or loving actions; or moral/ethical virtues; or loving virtues; or the new buzz-word "conscious", as in conscious change, conscious business, conscious leadership, conscious feminism, it doesn't matter.

Use whatever term or terms makes you happy based on whatever beliefs you hold dear, because they all relate to the very same *Me to We actions, attitudes,* and *ways of living and working in our world.* And all those different terms are all underpinned with the same moral or ethical or conscious virtues as shown in the following figure.

LOVING/CONSCIOUS ACTIONS ~ ETHICAL VIRTUES

These moral virtues/conscious actions include, but are not limited to:

Empathy, Equality, Respect, Trust, Compassion, Truthfulness, Fairness, Gratitude, Altruism, Kindness, Co-operation, Justice, Giving, Mercy, Peace, Joy, Acceptance, Non-judgement, Sharing, Patience, Courtesy, Generosity, Benevolence, Courage, Temperance, Nurturing, Honesty, Humility, Self-love, Self-control, Ethical/Conscious Sustainability, and Me to We—Conscious Living

And if you don't believe that it could be the power of the two that's behind these changes, that's fine. Because no matter what label you prefer, you can still work towards Conscious Change at home, at work, and across this beautiful planet of ours.

Then if you ever change your mind about the power of the two, it will still be there as an added bonus helping and supporting every conscious change you choose to make in your life.

Nevertheless in the pages ahead, as a reminder that all those terms mean the same thing, from time to time I'll use all those different terms interchangeably at different times as appropriate, because I'm not attached to any one particular term. I'm just attached, very attached, to the outcome – a positive, loving, peaceful, and sustainable world.

How about you?

And as I explain in my book, *Conscious Love*, by definition, any loving *virtue* is only a virtue if it's been habituated and so performed unconditionally, 24/7 as appropriate, because it's become a character trait.

However, if you continue to consciously repeat a *loving action*, eventually it will become habituated. And when it does it can then be officially called a *virtue*. And that's why, in this book, I prefer to use the term loving action or conscious action rather than ethical virtue, because the virtue status might not have yet been attained. But you can go out right now and start practicing any *loving action* you choose – and I hope you do ☺.

Therefore in essence, whether you want to see a more loving world or a more ethical world or a more conscious world, embracing the current rise in *positive* feminine-2-energy is the path to get us all there – women, men, and non-binary alike.

We really do have an amazing opportunity to attract that peaceful, ethical, loving and sustainable world that so many people ask for. All it takes is for us all to integrate those loving/conscious actions into our personal lives and our working lives, and spread them out into the world — "we're all in this together".

So let's now take a brief look at some pretty powerful historical evidence supporting the possibility that global consciousness does indeed have an energetic influence on the numbers associated with the year-decade-millennium.

And as you read through the following chapters, keep in mind that the global changes I speak about were automatically happening without anyone consciously working to enhance the current 2 energy. So just imagine the power the 2 could have if we all consciously lived in harmony with the 2 energetic-vibrations. Just imagine the beautifully positive affects it would have on your personal life, at home, at work, and in your community. Not only that, but if we all lived that way the effect we'd all have on the entire world would be incredible — global consciousness at work!

~ Chapter 7 ~
Enter a New Millennium— the year 1000 CE

When the water is stirred up by a storm,
the mud from the lake's bottom clouds it,
making it appear opaque.
But the nature of the water is not dirty.
When the storm passes, the mud settles and
the water is left clear once again.

~ The Dalai Lama ~

His Holiness, the Dalai Lama said January 1st 2000 would be just the same as December 31st 1999, and to a degree he was right. Nothing short of an environmental catastrophe happens overnight.

But we need to step back and look at the bigger picture and see the changes that might have taken place on either side of that significant date. Societal changes are a bit like a good novel, there's always a beginning, a middle, and an end. And so if you're looking at a specific date, there'll always be an overlap with the time before leading up to the specific date, and then the period of integration after that date.

In 1999 the book, *The Year 1000*, written by award-winning authors, and investigative journalists Robert Lacey and Danny Danziger, was published. No doubt it was published at that time to attract people who wondered what the year 2000 might bring.

The Year 1000 is a fascinating account of what life in England was like in and around the year 1000. What makes the book especially fascinating are the significant changes that occurred around that time — the end of one millennium and the beginning of the next.

It was around the year 1000 CE that the art of casuistry was introduced as the main form of ethical analysis and decision-making in the Western world. Casuistry (from the Latin *casus conscientiae* — cases of conscience) is about making ethical decisions based on previous ethical dilemmas and case studies. This is similar to the Harvard Business School's Case Method of learning.

However in 1656, the scientist, mathematician, and philosopher, Blaise Pascal (1623-1662) notoriously discredited casuistry for, what I argue, were totally unethical reasons.

Again, around the turn of that millennium, the metaphoric battle between Christians and Pagans was won by the Christians and Christianity began to take a major hold throughout Europe. As a result, by the year 1000 people were no longer buried with a whole lot of goodies for the after-life.

Around the year 1000, the abacus was introduced to England as was the use of a zero and infinity. And Arabic numbers began to replace Roman numerals. As Lacey and Danziger amusingly highlight, adding MCXIV to CCXCIII was not an easy task.

Interestingly, the new millennium also saw an increasingly organised system of government in England; poetry and stories began to be written down instead of just being learned by heart and passed on orally; and sugar cane was introduced as the sweetener of the day. Prior to that, honey was always used to sweeten things.

And of course, it was in 1066 that the Battle of Hastings was won by the then Norman-French Duke of Normandy, William the Conqueror, and this began the current line of English monarchs.

But the lead-up to the 1066 battle began at the very beginning of the new millennium, in 1002. It was then that disputes over royal succession began when Richard II, who was then the Duke of Normandy, arranged for his sister, Emma, to marry King Æthelred II of England. This marriage gave the grandson of Richard II, who became William the Conqueror, the grounds to actually claim the throne of England after he'd won the Battle of Hastings.

Were all these, and many other changes that occurred at that auspicious time purely coincidently?

Again I ask, how many times does a coincidence have to occur before that coincidence is given some legitimate credence?

Or is it at least possible that the cosmic energy of the new- 1- millennium had been influenced by the quantum theory of the global consciousness of the day? The same applies to the 4 in the 1940s, and the 5 in the 1950s, 6 in the 1960s, and even more so with the 2 being the millennium number in the 2000s.

~ Chapter 8 ~
Forecasts for the Year 2000 and Beyond

Promises are the uniquely human way of ordering the future, making it predictable and reliable to the extent that this is humanly possible.
~ Hannah Arendt ~

A gain, keep in mind that I wrote "The Power of Two" paper in the 1980s and so my comments about the year 2000 and beyond were pure speculation. But this is basically what I said and why.

You'll recall that the number one is said to be a left-brain, masculine number that promotes masculine *energy*. Again, not necessarily men, but *masculine-energy*; so attitudes, actions, and mind-sets such as independence, control, domination, and so on.

By contrast, as you're aware just like the moon and water relate to feminine-energy, the number two is also the symbolic number of right-brain, positive feminine-*energy* with the key words including peacemaker, partnerships, co-operation, *et cetera*. Again too, all key words relating to conscious change.

Nevertheless, it's important to highlight a significant distinction.

While masculine-energy and feminine-energy born of a range of sources including cultural and childhood conditioning can exhibit both positive as well as negative traits, the actual cosmic vibrations for the number two only reflect the pure positive feminine traits. These traits however, can be used in a positive or a negative way.

As an example, while the number two promotes partnerships, those partnerships could end up being either positive or negative. Similarly, the number two might enhance acts of consideration. But if the particular person allows her *negative* feminine traits to come to the fore, she might use the act of consideration in a manipulative manner.

So while the vibrations of the number two's energy are pure, it's up to the individual human to use those pure vibrations or characteristics in a positive way. And whether those pure vibrations are demonstrated in a negative or positive way will normally depend on how spiritually evolved the person is. And this is where love-in-action/*conscious* change comes in.

Anyone with a genuine ethical love-in-action consciousness will ensure that the cosmic energy of the number two is demonstrated in its pure positive way, as much as possible.

A Millennium's Dominant Number

During the entire 1000 millennium — 1000CE to 1999CE — the dominant, prevailing number was a continuous number one. So even though the decade-number influenced the year-to-year trends, such as the coming together and celebrations of peace in the 1920s after the end of World War I, and the focus on money and business in the 1980s, these decades were still underpinned with masculine-energy from the dominating *one* millennium. The man was the boss—of everything; of countries, politics, businesses, and the home.

This dominating, command and control energy led to generations of blinkered thinking that said: "We do it this way because this is how *I* say it's done—no arguments". Definitely Me not We. This is clearly a left-brain, follow-the-rules, fixed perspective, number 1 at work—negative Me not We.

My 1980s Paper "The Power of Two"

So briefly, in the 1980s my forecast for 2000 and beyond went like this. With two being the number of the female and promoting feminine-energy, from around the year 2000, we'd begin to see a major change in all socio-cultural aspects of the world.

I suggested that the years 2000+/- to around 2009+/- would be quite chaotic as major changes began to emerge and the old energies associated with the masculine 1000 millennium were still trying to hang on in their death-throes.

So what do we get in the following decade, 2010 to 2019? We get the return of that masculine **1** number-decade again. And so during that decade, the decade just finished, I suggested, back in the 1980s, that we'd see areas of masculine resurgence before all of that would start to be energetically defeated with the arrival of a double two with the year, 2020.

And except perhaps for the year 202**1**, from 2020 until 2100 when the masculine will return in some form for 100 years, we'll have a pretty fantastic eighty years. And who knows, with the attributes of the feminine two energy so firmly embedded by the year 2**1**00, we might find a new less dominating form of masculine-energy at play—more like Conscious Masculinity (see Chapter 17).

This could especially be the case because the two in the 2000 will still be the main prevailing trend. Although only the very young reading this are likely to be around to find out.

The other thing to keep in mind about 2020 and beyond is that the babies born in and around the year 2000 and beyond — our Gen Zs — will be reaching adulthood by 2020. By that time, most will be ready to mould society with their softer, peaceful, co-operative, yet assertive as opposed to aggressive nature, and dare I say loving actions and values resulting from the influence of the energetic 2 vibrations at the time of their birth.

Even so, just one important reminder. Again, short of an environmental disaster, nothing happens overnight and so the full effects of the feminine-energy will take over gradually from 2020. But after 2021, it will definitely be full steam ahead. And just think how beautiful the babies born in 2022 will be as adults. They'll be incredible.

Basically though, it's essential for men to develop their so-called feminine side at this time if they're to succeed in any and all areas of their life so they'll be in harmony with the millennium of the 2000s. Or put another way for those still skeptical about the power of the two. For men to succeed they'll need to develop their so-called feminine side to be in harmony with the ever-growing global *conscious* culture.

Similarly, it's essential that if women are to succeed, they too must demonstrate their *feminine*-energy and not be fooled by the erroneous and now out-dated belief that they have to act like men to succeed. That was a 1000 millennium belief that is not at all appropriate in our conscious 2000 world.

So that's what I said back in the 1980s. Let's see how that all played out by taking a look at what has happened in our world since the start of our new millennium, plus or minus a few years. Have there been any significant changes so far like those I fore-saw, and like there were at the start of the 1000s?

Around the Year 2000

As the year 1000 approached, many people feared the end of the world was nigh and so there was a major increase in the writing of wills. Now if they all thought the world was going to end, I'm not sure why they thought a will was even necessary. Nevertheless, a similar "end of the world" fear happened with the approach of the year 2000, but for very different reasons.

The Fears of Y2K

The first event to strike fear into the hearts of all worldwide was the Y2K bug, which after the event was laughed off as the biggest farce around.

Depending on your age, you'd be aware that the world was terrified of what might happen on the stroke of midnight on December 31st, 1999/January 1st, 2000 because so many computers had not been set up to click over to the year 2000, but instead would revert to 1900. And as everything in the world, from aeroplanes, to automatic teller machines, is operated by computers, everyone was preparing for the world to end, or some such disaster.

When nothing happened most of the world scoffed at how ridiculous it was for there to be such a carry-on over Y2K.

Now it always amazes me how so many normally intelligent people only ever take a superficial look at things and just go along with what the general crowd has to say—social constructionism at work.

And while I explain what social constructionism is all about in some of my other books, briefly its key defining sentence is: "When people talk to each other the world gets constructed".

Yes it's true that nothing happened at midnight when we entered the year 2000, but as I've always argued that's ONLY BECAUSE there *was* such a big carry-on about Y2K.

Because of the fear, or threat of a Y2K disaster, every business large and small, every service industry, every airline and bank, every computer company, virtually everyone who had a computer took massive action to upgrade their computer software so there would be a seamless transition from 1999 to 2000 — and so there was.

Yet those people who ridiculed the fears of Y2K as being a total farce, all 99.9% of the global population, actually make me very angry. And the reason is because it's yet another example of ignorance, arrogance, and superficial thinking at work that we see when it comes to so many important global issues like environmental matters (that I know I keep on mentioning). But see where we've ended up with environmental concerns.

It's more than just *important* to note that far from Y2K being a total farce, Y2K was the most fantastic example of what can happen when the *entire* world works together on a common problem — talk about diversity of participants all with a *unity of purpose*. It shows that no matter what country, no matter what religion, no matter what global fighting or wars are going on, it is indeed *possible* for the world to come together as one if the will is there.

So just take a minute to imagine what would be possible if, globally, we all focused on harnessing the power of the energies that the number 2 represents — the power of *conscious change*.

Surely something to keep in mind, don't you think?

Had the computer companies worldwide not supplied the correct updates; and had the world not spent an absolute fortune upgrading all their computer technology, who can really say what might have happened at midnight on December 31st, 1999/January 1st, 2000. There could well have been a global disaster. Aeroplanes might well have fallen out of the sky. Thankfully, we'll never know. All we do know for sure is that *massive global cooperative action* was taken and it was a *massive global success*.

So if you're one of the 99.9% who laugh at the carry-on over the Y2K bug, it wasn't my intention to offend you, but I do hope you'll reconsider your position.

The End of the Mayan Calendar

On more of a meta-physical level, there were the erroneous reports that the Mayan calendar said the world would end in December 2012.

As I wrote in great detail at the time on my old blog, the Mayan Calendar never made any such prediction, which is why my favourite cartoon at the time was the one above.

The Mayans did however accurately indicate that two major astronomical cycles would end around that time. But a specific date/time was open to debate. The first was the end of the 25,625-year-cycle known as the *precession of the equinoxes*, generally rounded out to 26,000 years.

The Maya and Aztecs divided these 25,625-year cycles by five cycles or world ages of 5125 years. The Hopi who also saw these astronomical events, divided the same time period into four world ages instead of five.

On this current occasion, as the major 25,625-year cycle is ending, so too is the 5125-year world age. So it was said that this time is unlike any other in the past roughly 26,000 years, plus or minus a few hundred or so years.

Now that *is* exciting. But it's a major difference to stating a specific December 2012 end of the world scenario.

Gregg Braden explores these cycles in his book *Fractal Time*, in which he speaks about many events that are happening these days that are remarkably similar to those that allegedly happened both 5125+/- years ago and also about 26,000+/- years ago.

As an example, just as today we're experiencing a decrease in the Earth's magnetic field, collapsing dynasties, multiple wars, and over extended economies; Braden suggests that there's evidence indicating that similar events were experienced around 5125 years ago. And with the exception of those last societal events because there were no civilizations as we now know them 26,000 odd years ago, Braden contends that 26,000-years ago the geophysical events at that time were apparently similar to what we're seeing today.

~ Chapter 9 ~
A World of Confusion in More Recent Times

Things are not always what they seem; the first appearance deceives many; the intelligence of a few perceives what has been carefully hidden.

~ Phaedrus ~
(c370BC)

In the Chapter-quote above, Phaedrus, the ancient Greek depicted by Plato in dialogue with Socrates, reminds us that "Things are not always what they seem; the first appearance deceives many ..."

And so as you read through this and the following chapters, I invite you to look deeper than just the actual superficial words on the page and description of the event. Keeping in mind the power of the rising feminine-2-energy — conscious change, take a metaphysical view and give some thought to what, as Phaedrus says, "has been carefully hidden" by the universe.

So let's start with an overview of our current confusing world that most people, understandably, view as being so negative and so confusing — but maybe it's not that bad.

If the energetic characteristics that the number 2, due to global consciousness, represents are actually at work in these various events, what could some of the seemingly very negative and confusing events actually be heralding?

When one of our Australian Prime Ministers first took office in 2015, he became known for his constant refrain: "There's never been a more exciting time to ...".

And he was right — well as far as the saying goes anyway. And that refrain can still apply, if we take the right perspective.

Setting aside COVID-19 that I address in Chapter 19, it's not just the great thinkers and visionaries, like those I interviewed, telling us that this is a time of change. We can now see these changes playing out every night on the television news, often in the strangest of ways.

We're in the midst of a world of global confusion and change. A time to "expect the unexpected", as many have warned. Although perhaps we should look at Oscar Wilde's full quote which was: "To expect the unexpected shows a thoroughly modern intellect".

So like Phaedrus, Wilde was also saying that only those with a "thoroughly modern intellect" will see beyond the superficial to what is actually happening, which could be totally unexpected.

During the second decade (2010-2019) of our new millennium, democratic countries worldwide found their citizens rejecting the traditional major political parties and traditional politics.

The 2016 US Presidential elections saw unprecedented support for Bernie Sanders on the far left and a non-politician in Donald Trump. Similarly, in the 2016 Australian Federal elections, for the first time 23% of the population completely turned their backs on the two major political parties and voted for small parties or independent candidates.

Yet three years later in the Australian 2019 federal election, those anomalies were completely reversed and the conservative party was returned with an overwhelming majority.

Meanwhile, the 2016 Austrian election also showed major unexpected changes with barely a hairs-breath between the far-right and the far-left candidates and the major mainstream parties didn't even get a look in. Not in the race. The same applied to the 2017 French Presidential election.

Spain went to the polls four times in four years, twice in 2019, because the people were so divided that none of the parties ever won enough seats to form a government. Although after the November 2019 election it seems as though a very uneasy coalition was agreed upon. But who can say how long that will last?

And in March 2020, Israel held its third election in twelve months, again because none of the parties had enough votes to form a majority government. Yet, Benjamin Netanyahu, who was elected Prime Minister for a fourth term in 2015, was formally indicted on criminal charges including bribery, fraud, and breach of trust, in November 2019. If convicted he could face up to 10 years in prison. Yet in the 2020 election he was returned for another term as Prime Minister. What were the people thinking!

And in December, 2019, the USA's President Donald Trump, became only the third American President to be impeached by the lower house.

To so many it all seems ridiculous, but people around the world are so sick of the over-rehearsed BS coming from the mouths of politicians. And in referring to it as BS, I don't want to appear crude. I'm just being factual. I could have used a far more refined word like rhetoric. But at least genuine rhetoric usually has some skill and merit.

However back to 2016, on June 30th Rodrigo Duterte was overwhelmingly elected President of the Philippines on the promise of cleaning up the country in the only way his very masculine-energy knew how. And he's doing it.

He proudly encouraged ordinary citizens to go out and shoot suspected drug offenders in the streets. And if innocent people got in the way and are killed, or should I say murdered, like the little five-year-old girl, Danica May Garcia, well that's too bad.

As horrific as that regime might seem to anyone reading a book like this, it's still a tremendous indication of how fed-up the people were with their previous unethical political system. It was a system that went by the name of democracy, but supported all sorts of crime, drugs, and corruption to the point that the people preferred a transparently murderous regime instead. *Amazing!*

Globally, from an economic perspective, surprises are occurring every day. In the United Kingdom, no one believed that the people would vote to leave the European Union — but they did. And if there's a controlling elite this would have frightened the heck out of them because it's a clear sign that the general public don't want to be controlled any longer by a controlling force — even if the European Union supposedly offered the UK as a whole, great economic benefits.

Then after the Brexit referendum there was a major outcry with masses of people wanting a second referendum. These were the people who didn't bother voting because they never believed it was possible that Brexit would ever get-up.

Yet in the 2019 UK election, when they had the opportunity of electing the Labour Party who promised to give them a second referendum, the Conservative party was elected with the greatest majority in 30 years. ***What the heck is going on!***

And while there are still many shocking physical acts of violence in regions like the Middle East, war has also taken on a brand-new dimension. Less obvious, but equally significant is the ever-increasing escalation of cyber warfare. Talk about a clean-hands approach to war. Not as many bloody deaths, but just as many overall long-term dire consequences.

No longer do budding terrorists need guns to perform acts of violence. All they need is a big white van and a boulevard filled with people to create mayhem.

But right around the world, as I'll talk about some more a little later, public protests are becoming a common event as people stand up and say "we're as mad as hell and we're not going to take this anymore.[16]"

As the moral philosopher, David Hume, said: "The general public always have the numbers and so the power to overturn any unjust act if they're willing to exercise that power." And the closer we got to 2020, the more people indeed exercised that power.

Yet on a community level, children think nothing of being rude to their teachers and bullying their class-mates to the point of suicide. What has become of our world when anonymous trolls can get their jollies by posting shocking comments on social media [negative-masculine energy at its worst]? Comments that result in someone's death. Surely, that deserves a manslaughter charge at the least.

One of the most poignant videos around is that of Amanda Todd who after being cyber-bullied, produced a YouTube video.[17] Four hours later she killed herself.

Another one of the many victims of cyber-bullying was Australian model and media personality, Charlotte Dawson, who was shockingly bullied via social media in 2012. She was saved from suicide at the last minute by a friend.

Courageously, Charlotte then used her public profile to expose the trauma caused by cyber-bullying and so-called trolls. However the bullying continued with the bullies and trolls winning in the end. In February 2014, Charlotte was found in her apartment, dead. She'd taken her own life. And this is still happening every day. *It's got to stop!* And hopefully it will stop shortly the more we all focus on positive feminine-energy and conscious change.

The Face of Climate Change

Oh, and don't forget the massive changes in climatic events, as I keep mentioning, arguably due to negative masculine-energy at work. Hundred-year hurricanes, cyclones, wild fires, floods, and famines are happening almost every year now. And the worst is yet to come.

Due to unprecedented heat, years of drought, and unparalleled weather patterns that have been attributed to climate change, the Eastern side of Australia was on fire, literally on fire.

Our bush [wild] fire season doesn't normally start until November, but last year, in 2019, it began in September. Hundreds and hundreds of fires were burning continuously for over five months, emitting around 434 million tonnes of carbon dioxide into the atmosphere.

Over twelve million hectares of land was destroyed, thousands of homes lost, thirty-three people died, and 11.3 million Australian adults were physically affected by smoke, during that period.

And there was a massive, massive, massive loss of native animals and farm animals—the estimate is that over three BILLION vertebrates were burned to death. However if you also include invertebrates then the estimate is around 240 billion[18].

In just two days in one region, an estimated 30,000 koalas were burned to death. Many koala colonies were burned to extinction. And due to unscrupulous human development, our beautiful little koalas are already fast becoming an endangered species. Scientists, and our chief fierys (fire officers) say we're to expect all that as our new normal.

But then the rains came.

And when they did they washed all the soot, ashes, and burned debris into the waterways poisoning all the water creatures from platypus to dragon-flies.

That's the face of climate change!!!

Now it's coronavirus (COVID-19) and the accompanying predicted global economic recession that I write about in Chapter 19.

Meanwhile, even Robinson Crusoe living on a remote island in the middle of the Pacific Ocean, especially if that island's name was Guam and North Korea had it lined up for a missile strike, would be saying: "Bloody Hell, the world's gone to hell in a handbasket".

To use a good old Australian saying that I grew up with: People world-wide are running around like headless chooks. [read: either confused or frightened, or both—and a chook is an Australian term for an adult chicken].

So is this all just life as usual from now on? Or has the global percolator reached boiling point and it's now time for us to extinguish the heat and pour that global cup of coffee so we can all relax and reflect on a happier, more loving, conscious, future world?

But even more significant than the current negativity and confusion, are the many specific on-going events since the beginning of the new millennium. Events that demonstrate the decline in the negative masculine and rise of the feminine, as I suggested back in the 1980s would be the case due to the influence of the arrival of our 2000-millennium.

Activity 1: Cpt 9—World Events Indicating Change

What major changes in the world, since 2000 +/- can you think of? You might like to make a note of them and keep adding to the list as more ideas come to mind and events happen.

How has your personal life played out +/- since the end of the 1990s?

There's normally an underlying metaphysical reason for it doing so. What do you think that might be?

~ Chapter 10 ~
Death-Throes of the Dominant Masculine-
Energy?

I want my sons to escape the pressure to be a particular kind of masculine that is so damaging to men and to the people around them.

~ Justin Trudeau ~

You'll recall that I suggested that especially during the second decade of this new millennium, when the masculine one number returned, we might see an increase in violence and negativity. This would be due to the waning masculine-energy of the 1000s doing all it could to hang on to its power and dominance, supported by the reappearance of the decade-number 1 during the years 2010 and 2019.

But the first decade of the 2000s was not without its brutality either, starting with the tragic events of September

11th, 2001, which to this very day are still surrounded in controversy.[19] And look at all the masculine ones in that date.

This 9/11 attack quickly led to an escalation of conflict in Afghanistan and the war in Iraq, which in turn ultimately led to the explosion of the activities of the terrorist organisation known by a couple of different names including the Islamic State of Iraq and Syria, or ISIS.

Equally as brutal, although not as bloody, December 2007 saw the start of what became known as the Global Financial Crisis (GFC), or in America, The Great Recession. And December 2007, is very strongly influenced by the forthcoming year, 200**8** that was only a matter of weeks away. And 8 is the number of money and business, positive and negative.

Born of unmitigated unethical greed, those behind the GFC demonstrated the absolute opposite of conscious business. If ever the world needed a reminder that a short-term, money-only focus just does not work, be it in business, politics, or any other aspect of life, it was the GFC.

This should have been sufficient to teach every business person on the planet to look beyond tomorrow's financial bottom line and their own back pockets and instead get with the conscious business program. Yet as most leading economists predicted, it would all happen again with far greater vengeance than anyone thought possible.[20] And today, that's what has indeed happened with the COVID recession.

In the late-1990s, I put together an adage for my business ethics and leadership MBA students that has always rung true and sums up ethical/unethical conduct. It certainly reflects the unethical conduct that resulted in the GFC/Great Recession and continues to reflect unethical conduct to this very day.

The adage goes like this:

Ethical actions can often entail short-term pain, but will always result in long-term gains.

> *By contrast, unethical actions frequently have short-term gains, which make them so attractive.*

> *But I guarantee that unethical actions will always result in some form of long-term pain and ultimate collapse, frequently in unexpected ways.*

At the beginning of 2020, pre-COVID, when I first wrote this version of this book I said: "The next global financial crisis could occur at any time. And when it does, (1) will it also be born of an unethical negative masculine-energy and arrogance at play? And (2) will it finally herald the last breath of negative masculine-energy and the final turning point to our new world? We'll see."

Well we didn't have to wait very long. I address those questions in the COVID Chapter 19.

Meanwhile masculine-energy was clearly demonstrated when we moved into the second decade of the 2000s.

In the year 20**11**, yes two more ones, we saw the very concerning rise to power of Kim Jong-un in North Korea; the start of the Egyptian uprising; the beginning of the Syrian conflict; and later the escalation of ISIS and their horrific terrorist activities worldwide.

Also in 2011, South Sudan gained its independence [masculine-energy], only to devolve into an on-going ethnic civil war [masculine-energy] with hundreds of thousands of people killed and millions displaced.

And on March **1**st, 20**1**8, we saw a great demonstration of negative masculine-energy in action with President Vladimir Putin's big announcement of his new nuclear weapons program.

Other current examples of leaders desperately hanging on to their negative masculine-energy because at some level of consciousness they know their power is in its death-throes include Putin's cling to power with his questionable 2018

Russian election win, and China's President Xi giving himself office for life.

And in 2017, Turkey's leader did a similar thing as have many Central Asian leaders including President Gurbanguly Berdimuhamedov of Turkmenistan and President Emomali Rahmon of Tajikistan. And of course, lifetime leadership is common place in any dictatorship, like North Korea and many countries on the African continent.

Many writers and journalists have heralded these events as the **"Rise of the Strongmen"**. Yet it's no such thing. Indeed, it's quite the opposite. You'll recall the words of Phaedrus who said that it's just "the intelligence of a few who perceive what has been carefully hidden".

There can be no greater demonstration of negative masculine-energy in its *death-throes* than these desperate ploys to cling to power at all costs.

Everyone knows that a playground bully is definitely not a "strongman". They are a bully because they are weak and at some level of consciousness they know it. And to compensate for their weakness they bully the vulnerable. These leaders are no different. They are just weak bullies doing all they can to hang onto power. Therefore please don't keep referring to them as "strongmen" — if indeed you do.

So will the disappearance of the power-*over*, masculine 1 number in 2022 see an end to these global atrocities and violations of human rights, together with the many other grabs for power?

We'll soon find out, although again transition of any kind normally doesn't happen overnight— there's always a lead-in overlap.

But that lead-in-overlap has begun.

In 2012 the United States signed into law the Magnitsky Act that is gaining global momentum. More and more countries are adopting Magnitsky-style laws that impose sanctions on foreign individuals who commit corrupt and human rights abuses.

This means that countries can retain a positive relationship with another country, yet they can impose various sanctions on that friendly country's individual corrupt and abusive citizens. These sanctions include such things as freezing the corrupt person's assets and so preventing them from hiding their ill-gotten money in a foreign country, through to banning their entry to countries who've adopted these laws.

Even so, as recently as a few years ago the people let these corrupt leaders get away with their unethical actions. But as I talk about in Chapter 13, the people are now saying "enough is enough—these unethical actions must stop". This really is conscious change in action.

So overall, do remember that the masculine-energy of the number 1 underpinned everything throughout the last millennium. And the number 1 focuses on me, me, me, as number one—the leader, power-*over*—as these so-called "strongmen" are demonstrating. Definitely me NOT we.

By contrast, the number 2 is about partnerships and relationships. So from the year 2000+/- the co-operative, feminine, power-*with* energy of the number 2 was at work starting to make its mark in parallel with the corruption, abuse, wars, and violence.

And here's a heads-up. This concept of the, me, me, me 1 in the 1000s versus the partnerships and relationships of the 2-energy in the 2000s is so important that I will definitely remind you of it again ☺.

~ Chapter 11 ~
The Rise of Feminine-Energy

Women could solve many of world's problems —
which men have caused

~ Barack Obama ~

Since the beginning of the 2000s, at the same time as we've seen the so-called "rise of the strongmen"—negative masculine-energy in its death throes—we've also seen the overt rise in the status of women—the rise of feminine-energy.

During this time, this feminine-energy has grown as evidenced by a greater emphasis on partnerships including same-sex marriages, co-operation, understanding, inclusion, emotional intelligence, balance—including work/life balance, and managing with a heart instead of command and control management.

You'll recall that those with strong feminine-energy—men, women, and non-binary alike—are usually more flexible; more creative; more caring; more compassionate; more sensitive communicators — all conscious characteristics. And so naturally, they also have a greater natural affinity with new trends in business, such as the introduction of conscious business and the virtual organisation.

Therefore again, it should be no surprise that the last twenty or so years has seen a marked increase in women in business at higher levels, as well as an increase in the number of female political leaders. Setting aside trades-"men", women own far more small businesses than do men, where creativity and flexibility are key. And we're even seeing a marked increase in trades-"women".

And surprise, surprise, internationally renowned economist, Dr. Riane Eisler calls this time the move from the Dominator Model to the Partnership Model.

It just *has* to be the energy of the number two that's supporting women, feminine-energy, and conscious change, at this time like never before. This really is the time for women to step up and make a difference to their own world and the broader world around them, with the knowledge that the cosmic 2 energy will support them.

Another major global change that also has an emphasis on feminine-energy, is the rise of computers, the Internet, and social media, all of which began in the 1990s and continues to grow exponentially.

Now what's IT got to do with feminine-energy you might ask, especially as so-called computer "geeks" are generally thought to be young males?

And that might well be true. But maybe they're young males with a strong *feminine-energy*. As Phaedrus said: "Things are not always what they seem; the first appearance deceives many".

So let's take a look at the Internet from a different perspective. It's always important to take a deep multi-perspective approach to all things—Conscious Intelligence Competency ~ Step 7.

It goes without saying that the world continues to change as rapidly as the Internet grows.

These days we talk about businesses based on clicks not bricks; the virtual organisation and virtual staff; and Internet marketing with its e-books, e-classes, webinars, and Internet dating. Of course this mode of business means a lack of face-to-face interaction, and we might also be dealing with people far away, on the other side of the world.

As a result, research demonstrates that at the heart of long-term successful Internet and virtual operations are ethical virtues like trust, relationship building, peacemaking or conflict resolution skills, co-operation, emotionally intelligent communication skills, and the skills to be a conduit between people. All of which should be familiar to you by now as they are all characteristics of the number 2, positive feminine-energy, and also conscious activities.

And all of those characteristics are the foundations of an ethical, heart-centred approach to business, now referred to as conscious business that is nurtured by wholistic, right-brain, feminine-energy. Again, not necessarily women, but *feminine-energy—feminine-consciousness*.

Computers also mean that a task that was previously considered to be exclusively "women's work" by male dominated managers is now a thing of the past.

Male business managers used to have their pretty female secretary typing letters for them. And larger organisations even had a "typing pool" of pretty young women tapping away at a typewriter.

Instead, these days men think nothing of typing their own letters and memos (now known as email ☺). Or even Tweeting government policy in the middle of the night.

In addition, in any business associated with computers and the Internet, creative ways of thinking are not just encouraged, it's an essential skill — and also part of Conscious Intelligence Competency ~ Step 7.

And creativity is basically linked to the right-hemisphere of the brain, which is inherently far more naturally active in the feminine.

So if you're still clinging on to that masculine domination style of business, take note. Research shows that rational, intellectual intelligence, generally referred to as IQ, only accounts for about 20% of business success. The remaining 80% is made up of other things, which includes emotional intelligence, empathy, humility, and other right-brain skills like creativity, and the list goes on.

When we focus on the person, productivity increases and in turn, so too do the profits. This is a far more ethical approach to business and one perfectly suited to the application of love-in-action/ethics-in-action — Conscious   Intelligence Competency ~ Step 5. It's also in keeping with the left-brain/right-brain perspective where, as Iain McGilchrist put it, the left-brain is the "Emissary" to the right-brain which is the "Master".

Perhaps it's now time for the generic term "master" to be changed. But to what? Due to the domineering masculine-energy of the past, the term "mistress" also has very negative connotations.

Another example which epitomises positive feminine-energy in action is the very special NGO (Non-Governmental Organisation), "The Elders". It was the brain-child of entrepreneur Sir Richard Branson and musician Peter Gabriel, who in 2007 asked Nelson Mandela if he'd like to head the group.

Today it's a group of fourteen former world leaders including Kofi Annan (until his death in 2018), Gro Harlem

Brundtland, Mary Robinson, Ban Ki-moon, Desmond Tutu, and Jimmy Carter, all of whom have let go of any political or national agenda due to their age and wisdom.

And yes, they have around 1000 years of collective wisdom between them. This ensures they're able to listen to global problems in a heartfelt way, and where necessary, intervene and negotiate in global issues in a neutral, non-threatening manner. Positive feminine-energy is about listening, discussion, and conflict resolution, whereas masculine-energy is about an egocentric predilection to conflict, fighting, and wars.

One more interesting example of the current transition to feminine-energy emerged during the 2016 US Presidential Primaries. Film-maker and activist, Michael Moore, was asked why he thought a 74-year-old Jewish socialist, Bernie Sanders, was doing so well in the Presidential Primaries. Michael Moore[21] said: "It's all about the young people. Young people don't hate. They don't hate you because of the colour of your skin. They don't hate you if you're in love with someone of your own gender".

And when were many of these young people born? In and around the year 2000+/-. They are our beautiful and very special Gen Zs.

These young people, female, male, and non-binary, have greater positive feminine-energy than those before them. I don't think Michael Moore knew it at the time, but he was describing the epitome of positive feminine-energy in action in our number two millennium. He was describing Conscious Change Today.

And let's not forget the Arab Spring and the Occupy Movement, both of which were an indication of the feminine-energy trying to breakthrough but being knocked down by the dying breath of the masculine-energy desperately trying to cling to life.

A similar example of the feminine-energy trying to breakthrough in a masculine situation was seen the day after the inauguration of a very masculine-energy Donald Trump, as President of the US of A. We saw the feminine-energy of the global women's march in protest. And again, after masculine-energy Trump's 100th day in office was the feminine-energy global march for action on climate change which Trump doesn't believe is an issue. Well certainly not as important an issue as making money.

But as we now begin what could well be the time of the most significant positive conscious changes the world has seen in a thousand years, the beginning of the 2020s, let's take an even closer look at the rise of the feminine and decline of the negative masculine in the closing years leading up to 2020.

~ Chapter 12 ~
The Arrival of 2018

*When the power of love overcomes the love of power, the
world will know peace.*

~ Jimi Hendrix ~

Hardly a day goes by that I don't hear someone using
the old "hell in a handbasket" expression when
referring to the world at this time.

And they just want to curl up in a ball and hide away
from everything and complain.

While on the one hand I tend to agree with them, on the
other to me these comments are a further indication of our
exciting changing world, not our *negative* world.

If you've ever been on an extended juice fast you'd be
aware that the first day is okay, day two things are starting to
take their toll, and by day four you feel so bad that death seems
like a great option. Then something miraculous happens.
About day five you wake up suddenly feeling great and that
greatness increases, and increases, and increases.

The same thing happens if you have a boil or furuncle on
your body somewhere. Gradually the pain gets more and more

intense until the boil explodes. And immediately after the explosion, it's happy days again. Sure there's a bit of mopping up to do, but the excruciating pain has gone.

Well that's what's happening throughout the world today at an ever-increasing pace. In Chapter 19, I ask the question: Is COVID the metaphoric explosion of the boil and the recession the mopping up.

Since this book was originally published as part of a larger volume in mid-2017 the global rise of feminine-energy has continued, often behind the scenes, but at a rapidly increasing exponential rate. That's one of the reasons why I had to update the book and republish it. But the speed with which the world is changing has reached a break-neck rate and only weeks after the last version was published, COVID hit and this current revision was necessary.

It's a bit like the "Doomsday Clock" which keeps telling us we're only minutes, or at times even seconds, from Doomsday primarily as a result of nuclear weapons — quintessential negative masculine-energy. And so perhaps the ever-increasing global chaos at this time is further indication that Day 5 of our metaphoric juice fast, or the explosion of our boil, is nigh, or has indeed happened with COVID.

Yes, very exciting indeed.

So don't view the chaotic global events as negative. Instead I invite you to monitor the day-to-day events in your own local region, as well as globally. With the occurrence of what might seem like just another day-to-day event, it's essential to dig, dig, dig, beneath the surface for common patterns, themes, and trends, in good systemic fashion. These will be patterns demonstrating the rise of feminine-energy "conscious" attitudes and the decline of negative masculine-energy, attitudes, and actions.

Frequently these changes will take the form of the general public saying in some way, "enough is enough", we don't want businesses, institutions, society, government, or any other group or individual to continue to act in this unethical, anti-social way anymore.

And as I mentioned in Chapter 9, this was evident with the 2019 indictment of Israeli Prime Minister Netanyahu, and the impeachment of Donald Trump, to name but two of the many leaders having to face their public over unethical conduct. Both are examples of the co-operative, peaceful, egalitarian, values and characteristics of conscious, feminine-2-energy coming to the fore demanding an end to previously accepted, as opposed to acceptable, negative masculine-1-energy ways of doing things.

And in the mid-1980s this is exactly what the numerological patterns indicated to me would happen at this time.

In Appendix B you'll find a list of just some of the many examples that happened in 2018 alone. And in Appendix C, I list just some of the more significant trends of 2019.

Not only do these two lists reveal the speed with which these changes are occurring, but they're also an indication of the sorts of conscious chances to watch out for in your own world.

If you choose to read through these examples in Appendices, B and C, keep in mind that ethical or conscious behaviour, love-in-action, and the characteristics of positive feminine-2-energy are all exactly the same. You won't have to think like Aristotle to recognise the unethical negative masculine-1-based-energetic behaviour in some of these events, and/or the positive feminine-2-energy shining through in other events. Hopefully they'll all be obvious to you.

Meanwhile let's close out the second decade in our 2000-millennium with a quick review of 2019.

~ Chapter 13 ~
Now to 2019

*The general public always have the numbers and so the
power to overturn any unjust act if they're willing to
exercise that power.*

~ David Hume ~

T he more chaotic the world appears to become, the closer
we are to that Day 5 of the metaphoric Juice Fast, or less
seemly explosion of the now excruciatingly painful boil.

So I invite you to not only focus on the negative in the
world, but also on the increase in the positive. Although due to
our inherent Negativity Bias[22], we generally find it far easier to
focus on the negative. As a result, finding the positive might
take a little extra conscious effort — but it's well worth it.

If you think about all the various examples in the
previous chapters and Appendices B and C, you'll see that
often both the positive and the negative will show up in the
same event.

As an example, the general public are speaking up in
protest and saying in *our* world [positive feminine-energy]
corruption and the rise of so-called "strongmen" [negative
masculine-energy] are no longer acceptable [positive feminine-

energy]. So much so that major unprecedented actions and penalties are being imposed on the perpetrators of these unethical actions — the so-called strongmen — who are usually the leaders of their own country.

And if ever those public protests reached an all-time high, it was in 2019.

But before looking at the events of 2019, let's just take a broad look at the numbers 2 and 1 and 9 and see if what they represent is what would have been expected in 2019.

First, we have the two in its very powerful position as the number representing the millennium. So women and actions relating to conscious positive feminine-energy had to be prominent in 2019.

Next is the decade-number 1, the number that represents masculine-energy. And although it's had the previous thousand years to develop, in 2019 it's in a much less powerful position than the millennium number 2.

Even so, men who operate from a negative-masculine-energy perspective will still be clinging on to their old entrenched ways in a last-ditch attempt to remain relevant.

And most interesting of all is the 9, in 2019.

As the single-year-number, it tends to have a lesser influence than the other two numbers. But it's significance here can't be denied. The number nine generally tends to have aspects of the previous numbers, 1 to 8, all rolled in together. But the nine's most noteworthy feature is that it's the number of completion and endings and this will make the masculine-energy, already in its death-throes, cling on even more — which it's doing.

But as you'll recall, there's always an overlap from one year to the next, and this time from one decade into the next.

So in Appendix C you'll find a short list of some of the more significant trends demonstrating the rise in feminine-energy, the death-throes of negative masculine-energy, or both.

Meanwhile this chapter highlights the two most significant themes underpinning 2019—the global protests with people around the world saying "this is unacceptable in *our* world" and the dramatic world-wide increase in concern about climate change, both of which are very much all about positive feminine-energy—conscious change in action.

2019—the Year of Protest

There may be times when we are powerless to prevent injustice,
but there must never be a time when we fail to protest.
~ Elie Wiesel ~
Holocaust survivor and Nobel Laureate for Peace in 1986

You'll recall the words of the moral philosopher, David Hume, who said: "The general public always have the numbers and so the power to overturn any unjust act *if they're willing to exercise that power.*"[emphasis added]

And as you're aware, in the past women were culturally taught to be submissive and under the dominating control of the men in their lives. So too, the citizens of most nations accepted the dominating rules and laws of their government's leaders, all too many of whom were corrupt.

But "hey what can we do" the people would say. Even in small alleged democratic countries where so-called democratic elections were held on a regular basis, dictators were able to rig the system so they would never lose their power.

You'll recall in Chapter 10, I spoke about a number of leaders who rigged the system so that they became leaders of their country for life in a bid to retain their unethical power— classic examples of masculine-energy in its death-throes hanging on for dear life.

The most notable of these was China's Xi Jinping who is now General Secretary of the Communist Party, General Secretary of the Central Committee, Chairman of the Central Military Commission, and President (for life) of the People's Republic of China.

But in 2019, many people certainly did "exercise their power" with the greatest recurring trend for the year being community protests; the like of which I've never seen before and I've been a political "junkie" all my adult life.

During 2019, major protests occurred in France; Peru; India; Venezuela; Sudan; Iran; Algeria; Hong Kong; Poland; Russia; Zimbabwe; Indonesia; Iraq; Ecuador; Chile; Ethiopia; Bolivia; Colombia; and Lebanon.

And these weren't just a couple of kids in the street with a cardboard sign. These were groups of thousands, hundreds of thousands, and in the case of Hong Kong millions of people taking to the streets saying "enough is enough".

Some of the one million+ people protesting in Hong Kong - Photo: AP Photo/Kin Cheung

The greatest outcry was against political corruption leading to many leaders resigning as a result. Unjust laws, general anti-government concerns, and the demand for free and fair elections also brought the people out onto the streets, as well as one-off issues, like the non-binary march in Poland; and the demand for stronger penalties for the perpetrators of femicide due to domestic violence in France.

And of course, the lack of government action on climate change.

All great demonstrations against negative masculine-energy in action. All great demonstrations of people saying the time is now for us all to have a more ethical, peaceful, and sustainable society. The time is now for Conscious Change Today!

All great demonstrations of the epitome of the positive 2 feminine-energy in action — conscious change.

Extinction Rebellion

Extinction Rebellion describe themselves as "a global environmental movement with the stated aim of using nonviolent civil disobedience to compel government action to avoid tipping points in the climate system, biodiversity loss, and the risk of social and ecological collapse."

Although I don't agree with all their tactics, even so, how wonderful that, prior to COVID, Extinction Rebellion was making so many people world-wide sit up and give thought to climate change. How sad that it's so late in the day that this is happening and now that COVID has put a temporary halt to all progress.

Apart from studying the Power of Two, it was also in the early 1980s that I began speaking out about the dangers of climate change. But no one would listen to me. And that was a catalyst for me starting my university journey a few years later as a mature aged 1st year undergraduate student.

In the 1990s when I did most of my academic studies, I had to do two separate masters degrees—a Master of Arts in Applied Ethics, and a Master of Science in Environmental Management and Environmental Education—to prepare for a PhD in what was originally Sustainability Ethics.

Now look at what's happening—*WOW!* Sustainability and environmental subjects, full degrees, and even Professorial Chairs in Environmental Studies now abound in every university world-wide.

Not only do we have the Extinction Rebellion, as well as a great many other groups like 1 Million Women, and 350.org all speaking out about the need to take urgent against climate change. But we also have Greta!

So many of the protests that I've mentioned were clearly about feminine-energy finally speaking out against out-dated negative-masculine-energy in action. And the anti-climate change/environmental protests have exactly the same energetic roots.

There can be no greater demonstration of the *result* of negative masculine-energy in action than what we're now experiencing with climate change. And until COVID, with the support of the cosmic 2 feminine-energy, environmental voices were being heard.

Yet back in 1975 Rosemary Radford Ruether[23] wrote:

> Women must see that there can be no liberation for them and no solution to the ecological crisis within a society whose fundamental model of relationships continues to be one of domination. They must unite the demands of the women's movement with those of the ecological movement to envision a radical reshaping of the basic socioeconomic relations and the underlying values of this [modern industrial] society.

So in essence all those years ago, Ruether was saying that the very same socially constructed, conceptual frameworks — the beliefs, attitudes, values, assumptions — that are at the core of environmental degradation, and today climate change, are arguably also at the core of the oppression of women, and vice versa.

And so Ruether was suggesting that women and environmentalists would do well to unite and work together for a change in what was believed to be the underpinning attitudes, common to the oppression of them both.

But today, it's not women's *movements* joining environmentalists to promote changes that might help to mitigate climate change. It's the cosmic energy of the power of two, due to global consciousness, that's pressuring that environmental boil to explode and the time to take massive action is *NOW*.

And towards the end of 2019, as we approached 2020, who was it that led the environmental way, globally? Not a young man, who it could well have been. But a young Swedish, Gen Z, WOMAN — Greta Thunberg.

Greta

The TIME Person of the Year for 2019 was Greta Thunberg — "The Power of the Youth". And when was Greta born? January 3rd, 2003. And interestingly, in numerology you determine the area of a person's life destiny, sometimes called their Birth Force, or Life Lesson number, by adding all the numbers of their date of birth together. As an example, if their date of birth adds up to a 2, they'll probably have the gifts of a peacemaker; if it's a 5 they'll be a good communicator; if an 8 they'll be interested in money and business, and so on.

And what does Greta's date of birth add up to? $1 + 3 + 2 + 3 = 9$. And 9 as I mentioned earlier, contains vibrations of all the other numbers 1 to 8. It's the number of the philanthropist.

A person with the destiny or life lesson number of 9 is a lover of humanity and they are "at the peak of life's expression and must show others the way. They receive wisdom from above; thus they know that the true way to happiness is in the service of others."[24] Sounds about right for young Greta, don't you think?

Now allow me the indulgence of repeating something verbatim that I wrote earlier in the book, as it's one of the most important things to keep in mind. It was a paraphrase of what I'd written in the original "Power of Two" paper in the 1980s. It goes like this:

> The 2 of course relates to our current millennium, the 2000s. And the "power" is all about how that 2 has presumably empowered women and encouraged the rise of feminine-*energy*, not

femininity but feminine-*energy*, especially that found in those born around the year 2000 and beyond — our Gen Zs.

… The other thing to keep in mind about 2020 and beyond is that the babies born in and around the year 2000 and beyond — our Gen Zs — will be reaching adulthood by 2020. By that time, most will be ready to mould society with their softer, peaceful, co-operative, yet assertive as opposed to aggressive nature, and dare I say loving actions and values resulting from the influence of the energetic 2 vibrations at the time of their birth.

… And just think how beautiful the babies born in 2022 will be as adults. They'll be incredible.

And here is young Greta born in 2003, so "around the year 2000". Also born around that same time were those inspiring young high school students who led the anti-gun protests in America after the senseless mass shooting at the Majory Stoneman Douglas High School in Parkdale, Florida in February, 2018.

So far the patterns and trends reflecting the power of the 2 are right on track and the boil, the furuncle, is getting bigger and bigger. And with the addition of climate change, definitely more and more painful.

Will it burst in 2020? Has it already burst with the coronavirus? Or will the pain continue until 2022+? You can read what I have to say about that in — Chapter 21 ~ "2020 and Beyond"

So as well as continually watching out for more examples of conscious change and feminine-energy in action, both negative and positive feminine-energy, I also invite you to do the following activity.

Activity 2: Cpt 13—What Trends are You Noticing?

Set up a list that you can keep adding to every time you see or hear any of the following.

1. Anytime you see on a TV program, or the news, or hear about an event that demonstrates positive feminine-energy in action—be it from a man, a woman, or non-binary;

2. Or that demonstrates negative masculine-energy in action—be it from a man, a woman, or non-binary;

3. Or that demonstrates the rise of the feminine or decline of the negative masculine.

~ Chapter 14 ~
"The Silence Breakers"
~ #MeToo

Men are afraid that women will laugh at them. Women are afraid that men will kill them.
~ Margaret Atwood ~

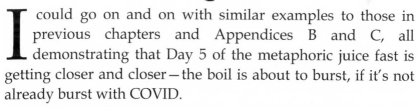

I could go on and on with similar examples to those in previous chapters and Appendices B and C, all demonstrating that Day 5 of the metaphoric juice fast is getting closer and closer—the boil is about to burst, if it's not already burst with COVID.

Yet arguably the single greatest *on-going* global acknowledgement of the rise of feminine-energy and corresponding decline of negative-masculine-energy occurred back in October, 2017. It was the #MeToo Movement and TIME Magazine making "The Silence Breakers", the Person of the Year for 2017.

#MeToo Overview

In case for some strange reason you missed it, let me just give you a brief #MeToo overview.

The #MeToo hashtag was set up in 2006 by Tarana Burke, the founder of a non-profit organisation that helps survivors of sexual violence. However, it really made its presence felt on October 3rd, 2017, after *The New York Times* published the story detailing allegations of decades of sexual abuse perpetrated by the American film producer, Harvey Weinstein. It was then that the hashtag came to life. Within 48 hours the story led to over a million people Tweeting on the #MeToo that yes, they too had experienced something similar in their particular workplace.

Within a week, versions of #MeToo in various languages had spread to eighty-five countries in all corners of the globe. Teams of journalists all over the world were starting to investigate similar allegations, from thousands of women, about possible long-term perpetrators of inappropriate behaviour in their own countries. Some of these allegations went back as far as seventy-five years in one particular case.

So what's really happening here?

In relatively recent years voices against domestic violence have also been growing in volume and are finally being listened to. This is both wonderful and indicative of the rising power of the feminine voice in this new millennium.

Indeed, as you would have read in the previous chapter, some of the major protests in 2019 in France were due to the growing concern over what they beautifully referred to as "femicide" — the murder of a woman — as opposed to the more familiar and generic term, homicide.

But no one ever seemed to listen to the voices attempting to speak up about inappropriate behaviour in the workplace, until #MeToo.

These abusive acts were mainly, although certainly not exclusively, perpetrated by men against women with the perpetrators being people exerting their control over others in a bid to satisfy their own egocentric, hedonistic desires.

And all of the inappropriate behaviour highlighted by the #MeToo movement is very negative masculine-*energy* behaviour whether perpetrated by a man, a woman, or someone identifying as non-binary.

Nevertheless, the forms of inappropriate behaviour range from bullying to abusive and inappropriate language and touching through to criminal acts including alleged deprivation of liberty and alleged rape. As a result, many people are saying; "well a pat on the bottom is really okay, but rape is a real no, no".

But if a pat on the bottom is really okay, this then begs the question: Would that same male perpetrator pat their female CEO, or Chair of the Board on the butt? I think not. So why do it to a vulnerable subordinate? It's all about egocentric, hedonistic, arrogant, power-over, control, and domination — all outdated negative 1000-millennium masculine-energy at its worst.

The #MeToo Movement has indeed changed our world in so many ways. It's certainly had a major effect on the attitudes and conversations of many men. Something I talk more about in Chapter 17 — Conscious Masculinity.

But the ripples have extended to unprecedented corners of society. Here's just one example I recently heard about.

A restaurant critic, was confronted with a major ethical dilemma. The food, the atmosphere, and the service in a particular restaurant was first class. But it was well known that the male chef's conduct, especially towards the female staff, was not only verbally abusive, as is often the case with many chef's, but he was also a sexual predator.

So what should the reviewer write? Great food but keep away from the chef? And then open themselves up to a lawsuit for defamation. Or should the reviewer just ignore the backend of the establishment and promote the great frontend food and service, which means the backend unacceptable behaviour continues?

Activity 3: Cpt 14—What Have You Encountered?

Have you heard of, or experienced, any unusual ways #MeToo is affecting society, like that of the restaurant reviewer? If so, make a note, and give some thought to how the situation should be handled.

Also, send that example and your potential solution to me at Support@ConsciousChangeToday.com so I can share it with others.

~ PART TWO ~
LIVING
A CONSCIOUS LIFE
TODAY

Having reviewed many examples over the past couple of decades of the rise of feminine-energy and so the rise in conscious change, it's now time to explore what living a conscious life in today's world might be like.

You'll discover what conscious feminism and conscious masculinity entails and why it's important. There's also a suggested guide for transforming our out-dated patriarchal culture into one of total equality.

It's then time to look at the links, on a number of different levels, between the rise in feminine-energy, COVID, and Climate Change.

Finally you'll find a guide for becoming a Conscious Leader of Change and living a conscious life in our ever-changing world.

~ Chapter 15 ~
Has #MeToo Gone Too Far?

*When will our consciences grow so tender that we will
act to prevent human misery rather than avenge it?*

~ Eleanor Roosevelt ~

Today, from a spiritual, or cosmic, or quantum
perspective, the 2 energy is all about peace, partnership,
harmony, and love-in-action/ethics-in-action and
cooperation—conscious change.

It was those and all of the other moral virtues that great
philosophers like Aristotle, David Hume, and Adam Smith
said were the foundation of an ethical way to act, an ethical
personal character, and an ethical world.

And as both Smith and Hume agreed, when someone
continually strives to demonstrate virtuous or loving character
traits, especially empathy and those loving actions associated
with bettering humanity, the more likely we are to see a world
in harmony with peace, love, and understanding.

So in essence, how lucky are we to be living at a time when the universe, the cosmos, quantum global consciousness, call it whatever you like, is giving us the energy and power of the number 2 with our new 2000-millennium. And with that global consciousness-initiated number 2 energy, the potential to cultivate a consciousness of peace, love, and understanding when we engage in Conscious Change Today.

It's true that those beautiful Gen Z people are being born into this energy and so for most of them, living a loving life will be instinctive and so a priority for them, depending on the type of childhood conditioning they experienced. And this concerning issue of childhood conditioning is something I discuss at length in my book *Conscious Self-Discovery: Enriching Your Relationship with Yourself*.

However for the rest of us, we have such a lot to learn even if we start from a foundation of instinctively living a conscious life centred around positive 2-based feminine-energy.

I was fortunate to acquire a great deal of this learning as I approached the year 2000 with the equivalent of around twelve years of full-time academic study at university. This included completing every Women's Study subject on offer at the time at the University of Queensland, as part of my doctoral research. These subjects were in fields as diverse as philosophy and social science through to English studies, history, political science, and more.

But it was serendipitously discovering the age-old field of moral philosophy and more specifically virtue ethics as an undergraduate student that really changed my life. As I wrote in more detail in *Conscious Intelligence Competencies*, I discovered that I'd been intuitively teaching others about conscious leadership, and conscious business, and conscious change for decades before the buzz-word "conscious" ever began buzzing.

That is why I'm so immensely honoured to be able to share some of those learnings with you here.

Even so, what I have to say in this chapter and throughout the rest of the book could possibly upset some women experiencing their newly energised feminine powers of change. So before I get started, I think it's appropriate to do what I do in most of my books and add a brief section that I always call "Transparency Time".

Whatever non-fiction you're reading, it's important to not only be aware of any credentials the author might have with regard to the topic, but also to be aware of any biases the author might have. These biases will generally stem from the author's cultural and family background, and *their life experience.*

Transparency Time

When it comes to a critique of #MeToo, and a discussion of what Conscious Feminism might look like, believe me, if anyone is qualified to give advice on this topic it's me. And that's not because of the alphabet soup after my name, although that has been of great help. But it's due to my life experience.

As you'll recall from Chapter 1, I was a disappointment to my parents for not being born a boy, and during a three-year marriage in my late twenties, I nearly lost my life on three separate occasions. And at a time when women's shelters and women's support groups were not known; and without the support of any family or close friends; my escape was a genuine "escape". An escape that I spent many months planning, saving, and preparing for.

In addition, in my early twenties I was abducted, restrained, and raped by a Catholic priest. And I've been physically attacked and beaten on a number of occasions.

I also know what it's like to be "victim-blamed" by people who've heard my story, but for whom words like compassion, or understanding, or insight were not remotely in their model of the world.

And you know what makes me so very angry about those who are so quick to "blame the victim"? And if you've been victim-blamed you'll no doubt agree with me.

Without exception those who blame the victim are those who've never known what it's like to be in a similar situation. Nevertheless they arrogantly and ignorantly have all the answers.

Harvey Weinstein's female attorney was asked if she'd ever been sexually abused. Indignantly she replied: "No, because I've never put myself in those situations!" Victim blaming at its best, or is that at its worst!

Oh and I also added my name to the #MeToo tweet having twice lost prize media jobs for not complying with the sexual desires of two different powerful male media executives. Indeed the last time, due to my non-compliance, the man concerned said that I'd never work in the industry again — and he made sure that I didn't.

And so due to my lived experience, I should be leading the charge to rid the entire planet of all men, as sadly many women claim they want to do in one (hopefully-metaphoric) form or another.

But I'm not one of them because my perspective comes with the wisdom of age and my great passion for a peaceful, ethical, and sustainable world—also due to my lived experience. The older you get, the more lived-experiences you acquire ☺.

As Aristotle said, the young cannot be expected to be prudent as they don't have the necessary life experience that only comes with age[25]. See there really are many benefits that come with aging.

My Greatest #MeToo Concerns

There are those who believe that many #MeToo supporters have gone too far in their claims, and indeed in questionably seeking revenge. My answer to the question: "Has #MeToo gone too far?" is both *Yes* and *No* based on a number of different perspectives. So let's just take a look at three of those positions.

(1) Culture Change

First, from the perspective of the need for major cultural change that is long overdue, #MeToo associated actions need to take things so much farther — but in an appropriate way.

The 2017 #MeToo Movement began due to women speaking up about abuse in the entertainment industry. Although *The New York Times* article did mention in passing that this was not exclusively an entertainment industry issue.

Of course we're all aware of the abuse against children perpetrated by members of the various religious and governmental child care organisations. What is less known is the sexual abuse by members of the church, especially the Catholic Church, against adult women too. Criminal abuse that I can personally attest to but for reasons too long to discuss here, I was not in a position to report.

Regularly on the nightly news I'm sure you like me have heard of one-off #MeToo types of abuse happening throughout all forms of business, industries, and professions. But occasionally this shines the light on another industry-cluster, as happened very recently in Australia with the law profession.

Women in the law profession began to come forward about the alleged inappropriate actions of a Judge no less, from our highest court in the land — the High Court, would you believe. When this happened, it opened the door for a closer look at yet another industry/profession with a pattern of bad and totally unacceptable behaviour, perpetrated by powerful senior men against vulnerable young women. Women who for a raft of reasons were unable to speak up about what was going on.

After all, in the legal profession, as with the entertainment industry and the religious hierarchy, and indeed most industries, this form of abuse was an open secret within the cohort.

So who does a young associate straight out of law school go to, to report being abused by a senior judge? Another judge? But can that "other judge" who knew all about what was happening be trusted to judge a *fellow* judge? *No!*

So what are we seeing here that must change?

Step 4 of my Conscious Intelligence Competency Framework is the competency of Systems Thinking. And thinking systemically, as opposed to systematically, is largely about the importance of looking for recurring patterns and trends.

What recurring patterns and trends do you consistently see in the above areas I've just mentioned?

Yes, I'm sure you picked them. The recurring patterns with all these abusive actions are:

A pattern of *predatory behaviour*; primarily *perpetrated by men against vulnerable women*; where there's a total *power and gender imbalance*; and virtually *no open-minded body or person for the women to report the abuse to.*

And as this predatory behaviour *knowingly occurs*; and *has been overlooked*; under the umbrella of a *patriarchal culture*; that has led to those *strong hierarchical systems*; that abusive culture and those systems are what needs to be changed — urgently.

And #MeToo is finally opening the doors and letting the light irrevocably shine on all these dirty dark, yet well-known secrets.

So from the perspective of the need for major cultural, patriarchal, and hierarchical gender-imbalanced change that is long overdue, I strongly thank the heavens for all the very courageous women that have led to #MeToo. And I believe that we need to take things so much farther — but in an appropriate way.

(2) The Revenge Seekers

A second perspective, however, that should be of concern to everyone is the view that now the #MeToo movement has opened its doors, too many women have falsely accused men of doing the wrong thing when the woman was just as much to blame.

As an example, this has often happened when a young woman is extremely flattered that an older high-profile or influential man is paying attention to her.

Now it's true, that the man might be over-stepping the bounds of decent conduct in today's #MeToo world. But even in relatively recent patriarchal years, his actions were not uncommon nor thought to be inappropriate. And so consensual activities might have occurred.

Then 10, 20, 40+ years later due to maturity, the woman reflects on what happened and calls it out as abuse.

Now it might not have been appropriate, but if *at the time* the woman was flattered or whatever and so *openly happy* to participate, *and she was not subject to any threats or had cause to fear retribution*, then, I'm afraid she just made a mistake. A mistake that with the benefit of maturity, yes, she might regret. But making mistakes is all part of growing up and no one deserves to be persecuted for someone else's mistake.

We all make mistakes of some kind and so must take responsibility for, and learn from, those mistakes.

Yet another perspective is that women have falsely accused men of doing the wrong thing when the man had absolutely nothing inappropriate in mind at all. This too should be of great concern to everyone.

Respect is a two-way deal. And just as men must learn to respect women, women must also learn to respect men and use common-sense to tell the difference between an inappropriate action and an innocent gesture. And this is why so many men just don't know what to do anymore.

As I'm sure you realise, it's a culturally common European practice, especially for the French, to give a kiss on each cheek, or even the triple kiss, when greeting someone (prior to COVID).

Americans are more likely to just shake hands (prior to COVID). While going back some decades before Australians were so influenced by American television, Australians would just greet each other with a side-ways nod of the head, a smile, and a "G'Day Mate".

So why is the triple kiss culturally acceptable but not a gentle touch on the back, as one high profile person was accused of doing many years before?

Yet since the start of the #MeToo movement I've read of a woman publicly shaming a man because he once touched the woman's knee. Another woman accused a man of gently stroking her back; and another of even just touching her back. Now in days gone by, many of those actions, especially the touch of the back, were also culturally appropriate signs of warm respect.

In the 1990s our then Prime Minister received some unwanted global publicity when he gently placed his forearm across the back of Queen Elizabeth. This was a culturally common way for a man to protectively guide a woman to wherever they were heading. But apparently Royal protocol says that no one is permitted to touch the Queen. But at the time, I can assure you that our Prime Minister was in no way sexually abusing the Queen, nor was he making sexual advances toward her. He was just acting in a way that was culturally respectful at that time.

And those last three words are key — at that time.

Unconscious Bias

This issue of changing times can be a real trap especially for people of "more mature years". These people have grown up with beliefs, and actions, and especially sayings that were thought to be funny, or endearing, or at least totally acceptable, forty, fifty, or sixty plus years ago. But today, they're totally unacceptable. Especially at this on-going time of #MeToo.

On a conscious level, the seventy-year-old might fight for equality and deny being in the least bit racist or sexist. Yet while a child is not born racist or sexist, as a child that person might very well have picked up and so use expressions from their parents that today are totally inappropriate.

So they'll still tell or laugh at a racist or sexist joke because when they were growing up, fifty years ago, it was thought to be funny, although it might still have hurt someone, even back then.

Or a man might refer to a young woman as Honey, or Darling, because fifty years ago it was considered a nice thing to say.

I know that when I'm at our off-leash puppy park, if a dog runs up to greet me and I don't know its name, I instinctively call it Sweetheart. And many other people at the park do the same thing. Now I'm in no way wanting a sexual relationship with that dog. It's just a term of endearment that was common-place when I was growing up.

If something like that is embedded in your non-conscious it's hard to stop innocently making that "mistake" unless, or until, the offensive term or action is brought out of the non-conscious and into our conscious-awareness.

I admit that it is true that instead of examining their unacceptable comments or responses, many people, especially those of more mature years, will complain about "political correctness".

So if you're ever offended by a comment that someone makes, it's up to you to politely say something to them and *explain* why it offends you. Don't just assume the worst. Don't just assume they're sexist or racist and then try to destroy their reputation or their career, as I've seen happen on more than one occasion.

Negative values and intentions versus automatic expressions coming from the non-conscious are two very different things. And that's why corporate training in the area of "unconscious bias" has rightly become such an important field in recent times?

The bottom line is that not every expression that upsets someone has a negative or inappropriate intent. And not every minor touch is, or ever was, sexual abuse or had a sexual intent.

People must learn to speak up, in a respectful way, if something offends them because the perpetrator of the action or saying might be totally oblivious to any wrong doing they might have committed.

However, if they are made aware of their offensive saying or action and they continue in the same way, that's a totally different thing.

In this world even today (well prior to COVID) some people, men, women, and non-binary alike, are inherently huggers, some are kissers, some are touchers, and other people are not at all demonstrative. In my own family my elder sister was definitely a hugger and a kisser, but for whatever reason I was never at all demonstrative.

Whether someone is demonstrative or not will normally depend on how they were brought up as a child. Or how many touchy-feely New Age/Human Potential workshops they've been to.

And what a sad (post-COVID) world if we ended up banning appropriate hugs and lovely feel-good compliments because some people can't, or don't want to, tell the difference between an appropriate hug and an inappropriate hug; or a well-meaning compliment and having someone hitting on you.

And there are very BIG differences.

By the same token, I know that on more than one occasion I've been rushing somewhere and I've accidently bumped into someone, both men and women, and when I did I accidently made contact with an "inappropriate" part of their body.

Now sure I apologised because it was a genuine accident. And I'd be surprised if you too have not done something similar at some time. Yet I'm seeing men being taken to court and publicly shamed by women who think the man needs to be destroyed for such an innocent "accident".

Again, if it happens repeatedly and you've spoken to the perpetrator about the action that makes you feel uncomfortable; then no, it's probably not an accident and they deserve to be publicly outed.

On the other hand, it is possible that a genuine accident has occurred and yet the woman has been genuinely traumatised by the event. In that case, instead of publicly destroying a man's career and reputation, again as I've seen wrongfully happen on more than one occasion, there's something a lot deeper going on for the woman that needs to be addressed. Perhaps for her own long-term happiness and well-being the woman needs to seek professional help to explore what's *really* going on for her.

Similarly, as I'll talk more about in the next chapter, many women sense this new power that has recently come to them but they don't know how to handle it. So they're using that power in totally inappropriate ways.

Sure in cases of abduction, rape, physical violence, and the like there can be no question that indeed a criminal act has been perpetrated and no matter how long ago it was, it needs to be called out and dealt with.

So just as men must learn that no, means no; today, women must also learn to *say* no at the time if something makes them feel uncomfortable — AND if they're in a position to say no.

Of course if they're not in a position to say no then that's another story that must be dealt with in a totally different way.

(3) The Victim-Blamers

That brings me to another side of the #MeToo debate that I find equally concerning — the victim-blamers.

All too many people ask why have all these women waited decades to speak up? And the answer to that question involves a very long list of reasons which includes: many women erroneously blamed themselves or questioned their own actions; many felt too ashamed; many women did speak up but were told to be quiet or you'll lose your job; many were paid to keep quiet; many were just not believed; and many who spoke up were then defamed.

After all, who is going to be believed, the powerful executive or the subordinate? Or one of the chief judges from the highest court of the land, or a young law graduate just out of university? And so many thought what's the point; and so the list continues.

In response I've heard arguments such as: Oh but these women asked for the attention; or were dressed inappropriately; or at the time they were flattered by the attention and happy to comply and now twenty years later they want to complain. All are victim-blaming comments from people who are either very naïve or obviously very lucky they have not been placed in that sort of situation, or both.

Another demonstration of great naivety and lack of empathy came from a woman mind you, who scoffed at those who said they'd lose their job, or miss out on their career-changing job, if they didn't go along with whatever the perpetrator wanted. She replied: "What sort of a woman would want to continue working for such a person"?

Clearly the answer is NO WOMAN. But if you have children to feed, or rent to pay, or no other opportunities, or are threatened with violence, the choices aren't always in your favour. The vast majority of women that TIME interviewed "expressed a crushing fear" of what would happen to them if they spoke up and complained.

But there we were in 2017, rapidly moving towards the 2020s with the feminine-energy window of opportunity bursting open. And it was then that some courageous women again stepped forward and this time they were eventually listened to by two very special *New York Times* journalists, Jodi Kantor and Megan Twohey. Is it purely coincidental that all that would finally happen at this very time.

Or is it the power of the two at work again? Who knows for sure? But I've never believed in coincidences.

So has #MeToo gone too far? In some cases yes and in other cases not nearly far enough—it all comes back to "appropriate" actions for us all in this 21st century.

And so in the next chapter I look at what could be considered the key characteristics of an appropriate form of positive feminine-energy-in-action—Conscious Feminism, followed by a discussion on positive masculinity—Conscious Masculinity.

After all, if we want to use this powerful feminine-2-energy — conscious-energy — to really make a difference to our world, as I hope we all do, then it's essential that we ensure that we're *all* using that power in a positive and *appropriate* manner. If we don't, we could ruin the entire opportunity that we have at this time.

Yet again, can it really be purely coincidental that this "conscious" movement really took hold with the arrival of our new millennium—2000+/- with its focus on the ethical, or loving, or virtuous, feminine-energy ways to act?

Therefore with so many debates about the pros and cons of #MeToo and the undeniable rise in the status of women and women's rights, the notion of *Conscious* Feminism is one of the most important forms of Conscious Change Today.

After all, as the status and power of women continues to rise, *and it will continue to rise*, it's essential for all women to think and act in what for many will be equally new, powerful, and appropriate ways.

Activity 4: Cpt 16—How Would You Describe Conscious Feminism

What do you think Conscious Feminism should entail? Make a note in your journal and keep adding and subtracting from your thoughts over time.

Feminism

Any *genuine* Conscious Feminist, whether they're a woman, a man, or identify as non-binary, *will* become a conscious leader of change. And when they do, they'll be adding meaning to their life. And there's nothing more important or more personally fulfilling and rewarding than to live a meaningful life.

But before getting on to "Conscious" Feminism, it's important to acknowledge the various forms of feminism that have made the notion of feminism and the feminist such polarizing and contentious topics over the years.

And over those years many different feminism labels have emerged including liberal feminism, Marxist feminism,

~ Chapter 16 ~
Conscious Feminism

*A feminist is anyone who recognizes the equality and
full humanity of women and men.*
~ **Gloria Steinem** ~

W hile the term "conscious" wasn't introduced into the
business literature until 2002, forms of conscious
business and conscious leadership were being used
and indeed taught throughout the later part of the 1900s.

As I mentioned in Chapter 1, in my role as Australia's
first female oil company representative in the early 1970s, I
instinctively used and taught all of my clients about what is
now known as conscious leadership and conscious business
practices. It was due to my conscious communication skills that
I won the top Australian talk-back broadcaster award in the
1980s. My doctoral thesis/dissertation could well have been
described as one in the field of conscious business or conscious
change. And naturally those same conscious business,
conscious leadership, and so conscious intelligence skills
formed the foundation of my MBA leadership classes in the
late 1990s/early 2000s.

radical feminism, socialist feminism, queer feminism, victim feminism, black feminism, indigenous feminism, and the list goes on, and on. All the various form of feminism have had the same underpinning aim of equality of the sexes, but with a focus on their particular area of interest. Unity in Diversity!

And before the arrival of our 21st century, perhaps it was necessary to have the many different areas of focus on equality. Although a great deal of the polarization in the feminism debate was due to so many different sectors competing for the spotlight.

Personally, with one exception that I'll talk about shortly, I've never called myself a "feminist" despite many of my life experiences teaching me that women were treated unfairly and unequally in the extreme.

Here's a very brief, simple, real-life story for the young, many of whom wonder why women my age make a big deal of female equality/inequality. This is just one simple everyday example of what it was like to live in those days, not so very long ago, when women had no rights in all too many areas.

In 1971, my then husband and I parted company and so I needed to buy a car of my own. As I had no money, I had to buy the car on an instalment plan — a hire-purchase agreement. It's at this point that women my age will have a big smile on their faces because they know exactly what's coming.

Despite being over the age of 21, and despite living on my own, as I was still legally married, the law of the day said that the hire-purchase agreement and the car registration had to be in the sole name of my *estranged* husband.

I continued to pay the car repayments every month without missing a payment. However after about two years my *estranged* husband decided he needed a car. And so he tracked me down and "stole" *my* vehicle.

When the police arrived and heard my side of the story they agreed that the situation was not at all fair. But as the car was registered in the name of my estranged husband, as was the hire-purchase agreement, as far as the law was concerned it was *his* car and there was nothing I could do about it.

In those days too, there was a minimum three year wait before I could start divorce proceedings. And so I had to wait until after the divorce before I could engage in any sort of legal agreement in my own name.

Needless to say, I've always spoken up for total equality. But I was never a fan of all the feminism divisions. To me that was a sign that each group was only concerned about themselves and not about women as a whole, which is where my concern has always been.

So surely in this new millennium the time has now arrived to empower women, all women, under the banner of an ethics-based notion of *conscious* feminism. It's conscious feminism that's all about wholistic, universal, equality no matter who you identify with—black, socialist, indigenous, liberal, queer, whomever.

Ecofeminism

I mentioned that due to the many divisions of feminism and my overarching concern with equality for all, I've never called myself a "feminist", with one exception. That exception is related to ecofeminism, which is actually a form of environmental philosophy with other fields like eco-spirituality, and deep ecology.

So would I call myself an ecofeminist? Maybe, maybe not. It would depend on the situation. But it's essential that I do mention it for two reasons.

(1) The first reason is for transparency reasons because one of the chapters in my doctoral dissertation/thesis was on ecofeminism, from an environmental philosophical perspective. The chapter is titled "The Magic Ingredient—A Relationship with Nature".

(2) The second and most important reason for mentioning ecofeminism in this chapter on conscious feminism is because ecofeminism could well be described as being directly related to, or a child of, conscious feminism in a number of different ways. I'll just mention two of the main ones.

A major difference between ecofeminism and other forms of feminism is that many other forms of feminism reject the acceptance of dualism when it comes to equality. The attitude for many is that women have been dominated and oppressed by men, so now it's time to reverse that situation—for women to dominate men.

But as you'll recall, throughout this entire book I've been saying that the rise in feminine-energy, and conscious change, is not about women being better or more important than men. It's about the attitudes, mindsets, and actions associated with masculine and feminine energy, whether you're a man, a woman, or identify as non-binary.

And most ecofeminists agree, it's not an either/or – men *or* women debate. Equality is equality—equality for all. The oppression of women is not from men but from patriarchal attitudes and it's those patriarchal attitudes and culture that must change—something I talk more about in the next two chapters. Having said that, it is true that those patriarchal attitudes are more likely to be expressed by men rather than women. But the distinction is important.

Keep in mind that any sort of "conscious" descriptor indicates that the topic must have an ethical foundation. And that conscious/ethics foundation includes the focus on equality and environmental sustainability, as part of overall ethical or conscious sustainability.

So at the heart of ecofeminism is the desire to bring attention to the potential that women have for generating environmental change. This comes from a belief that women are more likely to have an empathy with environmental degradation, exploitation, and oppression, because, rightly, of the similarities between those attitudes to nature, and the treatment of women.

Not only that, but due to the inherent nurturing nature of most women, they're more likely to care about the preservation of nature and the environment as a whole.

For some, this can come from a *human*-centred concern for nature. Although for most ecofeminists it's a nurturing concern for all of nature (of which humans are a part) from a *nature*-centred concern for nature—for nature's own sake.

Indeed it's the ethics theory, known as Ethics of Care, that comes from the ecofeminist movement.

A shining example of women joining together to care for nature and the environment is the organisation 1 Million Women — https://www.1millionwomen.com.au/

In 2009, the epitome of a Conscious Leader of Change, Australian Natalie Isaacs, founded 1 Million Women. Her aim was to recruit 1 Million Women and Girls from every corner of the planet and build a lifestyle revolution to fight the climate crisis.

And while I've never seen them link the movement to ecofeminism, but interestingly Francoise d'Eaubonne, who introduced the term ecofeminism to the world in 1974, did so in recognition of "women's potential to bring about an ecological revolution." A very similar aim to that of 1 Million Women.

However as 1 Million Women now has a membership of nearly 1 Million Women, perhaps it's time to change the name to 2 Million Women, especially in view of our new millennium, the 2000s and the powerful link the number 2 has to women.

The *Conscious* Part of Conscious Feminism

Conscious Feminism! What might that really look like?

As you well know by now, all genuine "conscious" activities are based on loving actions, or moral virtues as Aristotle called them. And when you have such a strong, ethically-based framework, it's easy to see what conscious feminism might be like.

Sure, continually increasing your overall levels of conscious intelligence is a good start. But that can take time.

So the first two steps, or competencies, to develop if you want to call yourself a "conscious" feminist — whether you're a man, a woman, or non-binary — are …

(1) Step 5 of the Conscious Intelligence Competency Framework — Ethics-in-Action. This is about habituating the most appropriate loving actions to your way of life.

(2) And Step 7 — Conscious Analysis. Develop the habit of thinking deeply about issues instead of just a superficial acceptance of things as they are, or as you've been told they are, perhaps (heaven forbid) purely on social media. And I'll talk more about these two specific keys in a moment.

But first let me briefly introduce you to the Conscious Intelligence Competency Framework.

Conscious Intelligence Competency Framework

We live in a world of relationships, both environmentally, and socially. And if you were ever in any doubt of that just reflect on the spread of the coronavirus.

And so peace and well-being are ground-up processes. It's all about ensuring you have positive relationships — at home, in the community, at work, and between nations. As a result, the key to raising your levels of conscious intelligence competencies is to have an awareness and an understanding that because we live in a world of relationships none of us can exist on our own.

The Conscious Intelligence Competency Framework can most easily be seen in the following figure that shows, first we have our relationship with ourselves. And often before we can make a difference to others or even go out and change the world, we might need to change ourselves first. That's what you'll find in **Steps 1 – 3** of the framework. From there we can develop positive relationships with others.

CONSCIOUS INTELLIGENCE COMPETENCIES

The Key is an *Awareness* and *Understanding* that
WE LIVE IN A WORLD OF RELATIONSHIPS

Your Relationship with ...

YOURSELF	OTHERS	THE WORLD
STEP 1 **Self-Awareness**	STEP 4 **Systems Thinking**	STEP 7 **Conscious Analysis** ➢ Critical Analysis ➢ Creative Thinking
STEP 2 **Selfless-Self-Love** ➢ Self-Compassion	STEP 5 **Ethics-in-Action**	STEP 8 **Spiritual Consciousness**
STEP 3 **Self-Control**	STEP 6 **Stakeholder Thinking**	STEP 9 **Ethical Sustainability** ➢ Environmental ➢ Social ➢ Economic & Political
Take Action ~ Make a Difference		

Step 4—Systems Thinking explains how everything in the physical world is interconnected—including us humans. Again, just reflect on COVID-19.

Everything is related to everything else. Everything is interconnected.

Therefore, to increase our conscious intelligence we need to develop the competency of Systems Thinking—thinking systemically (as opposed to systematically).

In other words, it's important to develop the habit of automatically thinking wholistically—looking at the whole system and how all its parts fit together instead of just looking for, or at, the individual parts. Examining the individual parts can come later, if necessary.

Step 5—Ethics-in-Action, in the very centre of the framework, is what underpins the entire notion of all genuinely "conscious" ways of doing things. These ethics-in-action virtues, as with all "conscious" ways of doing things, are all about *we not me*.

As I explained back in the last section of Chapter 6, ethics-in-action is about a mindset, and our actions, and attitudes, and ways of working and doing things and interacting in this world of ours. And it can go by many labels including ethics-in-action, love-in-action, loving actions, virtue ethics, moral actions, moral virtues, ethical virtues, positive feminine-energy, or the new buzz-word *conscious*—conscious virtues, conscious actions.

LOVING/CONSCIOUS ACTIONS ~ ETHICAL VIRTUES
These moral virtues/conscious actions include,
but are not limited to:
**Empathy, Equality, Respect, Trust, Compassion,
Truthfulness, Fairness, Gratitude, Altruism, Kindness,
Co-operation, Justice, Giving, Mercy, Peace, Joy,
Acceptance, Non-judgement, Sharing, Patience,
Courtesy, Generosity, Benevolence, Courage,
Temperance, Nurturing, Honesty, Humility, Self-love,
Self-control, Ethical/Conscious Sustainability, and
Me to We—Conscious Living**

And every time we come from the heart and demonstrate one of those loving ethical *me to we* virtues, we're making a difference to someone or something greater than our self. That then is the key to living a meaningful life, which is such a powerfully positive and rewarding thing to do.

Step 6 — Stakeholder Thinking is where we learn to recognise the pros and cons of how our actions and decisions might impact others, including the environment.

Step 7 — Conscious Analysis is the second essential step for the conscious feminist to develop. And so I'll talk more about this shortly.

Step 8 — Spiritual Consciousness looks at how being open to cosmic consciousness, or the universal mind, or quantum consciousness to name just three of many labels, can indeed expand and enrich all of our decisions.

Step 9 — Ethical Sustainability. In this step you'll explore the importance of our ethical relationship with all three arms of sustainability — the environment, the social, and the economic/political. So you'll gain an understanding of things that need to be changed in this world of ours to ensure peace, love, and sustainability in all areas.

While the linear step-by-step diagram of the Conscious Intelligence Competency Framework, on page 135, is easier to understand. It's important to remember that in systems thinking fashion, all nine steps are actually inter-related in a web-like network.

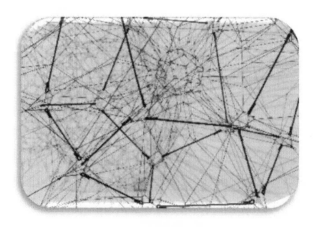

And competency, Step 5 — Ethics-in-Action, underpins all the other eight competencies. This is indicated in a very basic way in the oval image below. What that diagram does not show however, is that every one of the nine competencies is influenced by, and inter-acts with, all the other eight competencies just as all eight competencies, 1-4 and 6-9, are shown to be interconnected with Step 5 ~ Ethics-in-Action.

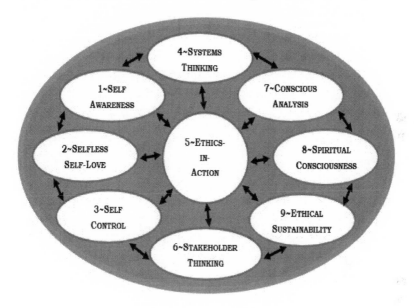

You can read all about these conscious intelligence competency steps in, *Conscious Intelligence Competencies: Taking Emotional Intelligence to the Next Level for Our 21st Century World of Relationships ~ with Yourself and Others, in Business, with the Planet, and Beyond* available soon on Amazon.

If you sign up to my mailing list I'll let you know as soon as it's out. Just go to
https://www.consciouschangetoday.com/subscribe/

The First Essential Competency

Now it's time to spend a little more time on the first of the two essential steps for the conscious feminist.

As Step 5—Ethics-in-Action is the foundation for all forms of "conscious" living, this is the competency to start habituating as soon as possible.

And don't just *look* at the list above of moral virtues/loving actions/positive feminine-energy characteristics, but actually study the list.

Then just choose a couple of loving actions from the list that most apply to your current way of life, relationships, and activities. Also make sure you include empathy on that list, said by so many including me, to be one of the most important moral virtues/loving actions of them all.

I suggest you do a Google search to find out what each of those particular chosen loving actions actually entail.

As a guide to the sort of information to look for, I have a number of *Essential Guides for Conscious Leaders of Change* that will be available early 2021 on Amazon. And two of them at this stage are on the virtues of (1) Empathy and also (2) Gratitude. So again, when you sign up to my mailing list I can let you know as soon as they are available. https://www.consciouschangetoday.com/subscribe/

Also in, *Conscious Love: Cultivating a Consciousness of Virtue-Based Love for a more Peaceful, Understanding, and Sustainable World*, I explore in more depth how to habituate, or integrate those loving actions into your life.

Now I'm sure that most of the time you do act in an empathic way, or act with kindness, or compassion. But be constantly on the alert for times when you might be triggered to not be as kind, or as compassionate as you could be.

Those are the times when you have to stop and really assess the situation. Because as I explain in *Conscious Love*, on rare occasions demonstrating ethics-in-action, a loving action, might not be the most appropriate thing to do.

Activity 5: Cpt 16—What Loving Actions Would You Choose?

Look through the list of loving actions in the image above and select the six that you would be most likely to use in your personal life, or at work. Then rank them in order of importance to your life's activities.

Are there any other loving actions/moral virtues not listed in the image that you can think of that would be important in the life you lead or the work you do? If so, list those and slot them into their priority ranking with the six you've already written down.

Now to the *Feminism* Part of Conscious Feminism

If the conscious part of being a conscious feminist is based on ethics-in-action — from Me to We — what is feminism about today, in our 21st century world?

Feminism has always been about striving for much needed greater rights for women. But today, it's better to look at feminism as working towards total equality for all.

You'll recall my discussion in Chapter 5 in which I spoke about both positive feminine-energy in action and negative-feminine-energy in action.

You can never claim to be a "conscious" feminist until you strive to demonstrate positive feminine-energy at virtually all times. And sure, there'll be times when set-backs occur. But it's then all about dusting yourself off and continuing to work to habituate those positive feminine-energy traits, those loving actions, those moral virtues, those conscious actions.

Genuine success and indeed excelling in the 2020s and beyond will be experienced when *positive* feminine-energy in women and *positive* masculine-energy in men are in balance like the Yin Yang symbol demonstrates. And this is something that many of our young, and not so young, #MeToo feminists are having trouble with.

In late 2019, a TV current affairs panel show was screened on Australia's national broadcaster. The show's topic was titled "Ageism, Violence Against Women, and Post #MeToo". The panel was made up of five so-called feminists and a moderator, who at times could not believe what she was encountering. It's true that a couple of the panellists were reasoned in their comments. But a couple, and one in particular, was not.

The show received so many complaints, that it was removed from the station's replay website. As a result, I could give you many examples of my concerns about the program. But the following example was the source of my greatest distress, because it demonstrates a growing view that is considered by some feminists as appropriate and totally acceptable. And it is not!

The question was asked:

"When trying to bring about significant change, when is aggression and violence a better option than assertiveness, strong arguments, and modelling the behaviour you expect of others?"

One woman answered: "When none of that other stuff works".

And from another woman: "... I want patriarchy to fear feminism. ... [because] nothing protects them [women] from patriarchy. ... as a feminist the most important thing is to destroy patriarchy and all of this talk about how, if you talk about violence, you're just becoming like the men. ... But how long must we wait for men and boys to stop murdering us, to stop beating us, and to stop raping us? How many rapists must we kill? ... As a woman I'm asking, how many rapists must we kill until men stop raping us?"

To which another woman on the panel added:

"There are many causes where people have resorted to violence as a way to finally break through and get heard and achieve what we need. And if that's what it takes, that's what it takes".

Now it's true that many of the points the various panellists raised were spot on. But declaring that the answer is violence until patriarchy is afraid of feminism is the exact opposite of the strength the conscious 2 energy and positive feminine-energy is giving us.

Calling for women to use violence is a sign of great fear and weakness, just as male violence is a major sign of great fear and weakness — definitely not strength. And I for one do not want to see women demonstrating any kind of weakness any more. That's a thing of that past.

If women use violence they are indeed demonstrating the exact same negative masculine-actions as those used by the men that they want to see disappear from the planet.

So no, violence is not the answer with one exception. If some man is beating the bejesus out of you, you run for your life or fight back in some form for all you're worth. After all, your life could depend on it. Then go and get help. Because no man who treats you like that loves you, no matter what he says. He might well have a dependent need for you to be around. But that's not love.

However from a societal perspective, violence is never the way to change the culture. It makes absolutely no sense at all, because once again you're just swapping masculine-weakness and fear in the form of violence for feminine-weakness and fear in the form of violence. You're just changing the perpetrator. You're not changing the act. You're not changing the culture.

For goodness sake, by definition it's **_violence, all violence_**, that must be stopped if we're to have a peaceful, loving, sustainable, and sane world.

When two opposing sides set out to kill each other that is what a war is all about. And war is not the answer to any situation. Surely we're a far more advanced and sophisticated society in this 21st century than that.

People like Gandhi and Martin Luther King Jr did not advocate war and killing each other and yet they were both the source of incredible cultural change.

It's interesting to note that the woman advocating killing the rapists was raped as a teenager. But I too was tied-up and raped as a young woman. And sadly that wasn't the worst thing to have happen to me at the hands of a man.

The woman on the TV show calling for violence and killing rapists was clearly extremely angry. And I too get angry at times — especially with victim-blamers as you know. And even Aristotle[26] said, anger is not necessarily a bad thing —

The person who gets angry at the right things and with the right people, and also in the right way and at the right time and for the right length of time, is commended.

Indeed, anger can be a great motivator of action to go out and make a difference.

But for action to be successful, that action must be *appropriate action* — something I talk more about in the final chapter of this book. And that anger must be appropriate anger.

So I say cultural change is essential, but it will never be effectively achieved with violence. In Chapter 18 I offer a number of ways that might help us move in the right direction.

After all — please remember what this book is all about. It's about acknowledging that, yes, those women on that panel were right in saying nothing has changed in the past. But please remember that that past was influenced by the 1000 millennium where men were supported by 1000 years of global consciousness on the 1 energies, to reign supreme and commit their acts of masculine, patriarchal violence.

Now with our new global consciousness-born, conscious 2 energies working their hardest to support us to bring about change; positive ethical conscious change. Let's give it a chance and start working in harmony *with* those conscious 2 energies, not *against* those conscious 2 energies.

Because if we women just start using the old out-dated negative masculine-energy in an attempt to bring about the change we want, then we women will also end up in our death-throes as that 1000-millennium 1 is extinguished.

We all have the most beautiful and wonderful opportunity to bring this change about in the right way with this new 2000-millennium. At least give it a chance.

Sure, before change fully takes place, more women will die at the hands of their male partners. And more women will be raped. And more women will be abused.

So we all need to start and work together without delay to ensure that the thought of those lost lives and those abused can persuade us even more about the urgent need for change.

But get that change to happen, not over more violence, but over long-term peace, understanding, and sustainability. It must be Conscious Change.

All too often I'm hearing women asserting their newly developing rights and empowerment. And as some of the women on the TV panel show demonstrated, they often don't know how to handle these new powers that they now have.

It's like putting a teenage boy from the city into a very powerful, first car. He doesn't know how to handle the vehicle itself nor the responsibility attached to having command of such a vehicle.

And that brings me to the second fundamental key to conscious feminism—depth! Or Conscious Intelligence Competency ~ Step 7—Conscious Analysis, which is largely about looking deeply into all the actions we take and the decisions we make.

Second Essential Competency—Conscious Analysis—Depth

Conscious Analysis, Step 7, has two components, Creative Thinking and Critical Analysis. The creative thinking helps you to come up with an ever-increasing number of ways to look at a situation that can then be critically analysed before a course of action is decided upon.

And Conscious Intelligence Competency ~ Step 6 — Stakeholder Thinking, will guide you when looking for those who might be affected by your decision and how they might be affected. So Critical Analysis is all about looking at things at deeper and deeper levels.

You'll recall that due to their superficial perspective, I said I got quite angry with those who ridiculed the fears of Y2K as being a total farce. When far from Y2K being a total farce, it was the most fantastic example of what can happen when the *entire* world works together on a common problem.

But unfortunately, most people do tend to look at situations from purely a superficial level. Hey, after all it's easier to do that. But if you want to call yourself a conscious feminist, or a conscious leader of change, then I'm sorry but that takes a little more effort than that.

There's a major part of environmental philosophy known as Deep Ecology. It was developed in the 1970s by a beautiful old Norwegian philosopher, who unfortunately is no longer with us. His name is Arne Naess.

And Professor Naess said that the problem with our natural environment is that most people only take a very shallow look at what is going on. So they only ever make very superficial changes that might well be misguided due to their superficial perspective.

He said if we have any hope of looking after nature and the environment then it's essential that on every occasion we take a much deeper multi-dimensional look at what's going on and the decisions that must be made to help the situation.

Indeed that is the very basis of philosophy itself and all philosophical arguments—to dig, dig, dig, as deeply into the issue as possible. It's essential to take a multi-perspective view at every turn, continually looking for the impacts, ramifications, unintended consequences, and implications of every proposed action and decision.

I don't know about where you live, but the number of times I've heard a politician announce a new government policy. Then shortly after, all sorts of problems arise that they hadn't expected. It's basic Scenario Planning 101 that politicians seem to never do, or if they do, they do it very badly.

Prince Harry and Meghan, the Duke and Duchess of Sussex, deciding they were going to make a fortune by selling merchandise under the Royal Sussex brand is another clear example of the negative results of not using conscious analysis when making a decision.

Let's just assume that the Queen had let them do it. Then, yes, they might have made a lot of money out of the Royal Sussex brand. But they obviously gave the idea virtually no thought past the first dollar sign.

And sure their Royal Sussex brand might have been intended to raise money for charitable endeavours—I don't know for sure. But to what extent is their lavish lifestyle also being funded by the money they're raising in the name of charity?

Not only that, but they clearly didn't even consider how the Queen might have felt about the idea—a total lack of the loving virtue of empathy. Next they didn't even consider how the people of the Commonwealth might react—again a total lack of empathy. They continually campaign for a more sustainable world yet crass commercialism funding a lavish lifestyle is often at the heart of global inequality. And I could go on and on.

So you have a couple of young people, at first demonstrating the epitome of positive 2 feminine-energy in action, as I mentioned in Appendix B. Now they have sullied their image and credibility in so many ways because of clearly not *consciously analysing,* at deeper and deeper levels, their decisions surrounding so-called going out on their own.

And while on the Royal family, Prince Andrew — the Queen's 3rd child — is another who demonstrated a great need to learn about conscious analysis after his disastrous BBC interview about his association with sex-offender, Jeffery Epstein.

A similar lack of conscious analysis is to say "so long as men keep killing and abusing women" then violence is acceptable, as the women on the TV panel suggested. That is such a very superficial approach — you punch me and I'll punch you. That's not the way to end cultural violence. Superficial approaches never work in the long-term.

With the increasing power of the 2 from our 2000-millennium, we have increasing responsibilities in how we handle that new power. That's why the Conscious Intelligence Competency ~ Step 7 — Conscious Analysis, is so vital to develop.

Activity 6: Cpt 16—Thinking About Stakeholders

Think about the most important feminist issue that you'd like to work on or think needs changing.

List in your journal as many stakeholders who might be affected by those changes. These could be individuals, or sectors of society, or even organisations.

Now thinking about ethics-in-action and the list of loving actions in the image several pages back versus various forms of violence.

1. Thinking critically, in general what are the pluses and minuses of acting in an ethical way versus a violent way to affect change in this situation.

2. Go through your list of relevant stakeholders that you wrote down, and make a few notes about the pluses and minuses for each of them of acting in an ethical versus a violent way.

3. What did you learn from this activity?

In Summary

So the conscious part of conscious feminism is all about striving to habituate positive feminine-energy actions/ethical virtues 100% of the time, when appropriate. This positive feminine-energy is another way of describing the Conscious Intelligence Competency ~ Step 5—Ethics-in-Action.

The feminism part is all about acknowledging that a feminist is anyone who recognizes the equality and full humanity of women, men, and non-binary. And this will be helped by continuing to dig, dig, dig, as deeply as possible into the ramifications and implications of any views, decisions, or actions. And Conscious Intelligence Competencies ~ Step 7—Conscious Analysis and also Step 6—Stakeholder Thinking will help you do that.

So while the rise in the status of women at this time is fantastic, it's essential that that rise doesn't grow excessively in a negative egocentric manner leading to the woman's desire to dominate and control men, or worse. That's not what living in harmony with the conscious 2 energy and success in the 2020s+ is all about.

Those attitudes and actions will not only be personally ruinous, but they'll work against all the beauty that the #2 energy is attempting to bring to the planet.

Therefore, it's essential that if women, and our world, are to excel, women must demonstrate their positive feminine-energy and not be fooled by the erroneous and antiquated 1000s millennium belief that they have to act like men to succeed. In these 2000s, that will not work.

Remember, the more of those ethics-in-action/loving actions you habituate, the more you'll be living in harmony with that 2 energy, and the more wonderfully enriched your personal life will become too.

And those loving actions will also help you mediate between your positive feminine-energy and any negative feminine-energy that might occasionally show up. They'll also help you mediate between the appropriate and inappropriate expressions of masculine-energy found in your feminine.

As I've said before, from a big-picture perspective the power of the two energy is all about supporting a more peaceful, loving, sustainable, and conscious world. And that, of course, includes a world where women, men, and non-binary are all equal.

But what has been happening to men since the #MeToo world arrived?

~ Chapter 17 ~
Conscious Masculinity

*Education is the passport to the future, for tomorrow
belongs to those who prepare for it today.*

~ Malcolm X ~

ॐ

U p until now, men had been taught to suppress their
feminine-energy, especially their emotions; just as
women were taught to suppress their masculine-
energy and just be submissive.

And you'll recall that masculine-energy is commonly
known for domination, control, power-over, independence,
impatience, aggression, individuality, and self-centred
ambition, all of which are considered moral vices these days.
Yet as I briefly indicated in Chapter 5, if we go back to caveperson times we'll see that those so-called negative masculine
traits had an important role to play.

An Evolutionary Perspective

In ancient times as you know, it was the women who had
the babies and so the men had to protect the mother and
children from bears and lions or whatever, and also provide a

lot of the major food supplies. And if the women didn't continue to have children the species would die out. Those same actions and concerns are beautifully displayed today in many non-human animals too.

So to perform their required masculine duties, the men of the past needed those common masculine traits. If he was going to compete for a mate and then protect his partner and children in those dangerous times, he needed to take charge, or take "control" of his family's activities to keep them safe from harm.

An analogy can be drawn between a loving parent whose duty it is to care for and protect their children. The parent needs to dominate, and control, and have power-over the child, albeit in an appropriate manner, so the child can be taught how to survive in the big, wide, world—especially our 21st century world.

Keeping those issues in mind, traits like domination, control, power-over and so forth are not so negative after all. So where did it all go wrong?

Times have Changed

The first problem comes with both the individual men, as well as society, seeing one type of trait as being *superior* to another type of trait. Because the man is generally known for his physical strength, larger stature, competitive abilities, preparedness and tendency to fight, control, and dominate, it was natural to see him as superior to the woman who just did what women naturally do—have babies, prepare the food, and talk amongst the other women and so need to be protected. Looking at the situation from that perspective it's not surprising that women were seen as inferior to men, even by women themselves.

Yet especially in today's world, as I've said on many occasions, competition, fighting, control, and domination, and all those other similar masculine traits are far from expressions of strength and superiority. These days those traits are expressions of enormous weakness.

Now that we don't generally have to worry about bears and lions and hunting for food, true power lies in positive *feminine-energy*, the greatest supporter of love consciousness, cooperation, and partnership. Because positive feminine-energy creates, nurtures, and sustains life in more ways than just having babies we're realising that without those feminine-energy traits, humans won't continue to flourish and grow in peace, harmony, and love.

These erroneous historical beliefs of seeing women as inferior to men are then combined with the escalation of negative masculine ego and the strong likelihood of negative childhood conditioning. The result is that with the man generally being physically stronger he believes that he must get even stronger to become more of a "man". He equates this strength with power and so must compete to continue to demonstrate how powerful he actually is. In other words, how much of a *real man* he actually is. And over time these attitudes continued to escalate, inappropriately both on an individual and well as a cultural level.

One clear example is best seen with many non-human animal species. The female selects the mate who she thinks is going to be the best father, protector, and provider. And so the masculine need to compete arises as the potential mate does all he can to demonstrate that he'll be a better mate than any other male around. And on it goes.

Yet while times change, that competitive, controlling evolutionary instinct is so strongly non-consciously embedded that if men today are to change with the changing times, they'll require some very hard work on a conscious level to retrain their brain.

Even moving from the caveperson times to the Middle Ages and up until the last hundred years or so society continued to see women as inferior little creatures. Therefore it was believed these so-called negative "protective" masculine traits still had an important role to play.

But today in the early 21st century, times have indeed changed. Women no longer need to be dominated as a means of keeping them safe because they're merely the source of future generations. And due to our commercialised world, not only do women want to work to give their life meaning, but they have to work to supplement the family income.

So times have changed as have some men, but a lot of men haven't.

Here we are in the 2000s with the undeniable rise of feminine-*energy*, of which the #MeToo movement is but one of many current-day examples. But it's #MeToo that's confusing the heck out of most men.

As a result, it's imperative at this time that men are not forgotten or categorically demeaned. Instead it's time that men are now taught about our new world and what is, and is not, appropriate action. And while that might sound a little patronising, it's not intended that way. It's just a statement of fact.

If I was to go out and expect to fly a plane, I'd need someone to teach me how to do that — just a statement of fact.

So it's imperative that men are helped to understand what's going on in our conscious changing world today. And it's imperative that they're shown the very positive side to living a new kind of life while, most importantly, still retaining their masculinity.

With the knowledge and understanding of how to act in a love-in-action/conscious way, in a love-in-action/conscious world, men will be able to become role-models for conscious change for other men and their sons.

Today women are celebrating the current changes because "Hey we now have the strength and courage to speak up about past injustices". Yet the opportunities for men at this time are both enormous and just as exciting if they choose to be open to them.

So where to start?

Characteristics for the 21st Century Man—*Conscious Masculinity*

For humanity to progress in a peaceful, understanding, and loving way, we still need a combination of masculine-energy and feminine-energy, working together in a balanced harmonious manner as the Yin Yang symbol demonstrates.

So despite the long-overdue rise of feminine-energy, we can't have a totally feminine-based society. And sure, just as we have black and white, and night and day, women will still have babies and men will still, generally, have greater body strength to lift heavy objects. But it comes back to the notion of oneness and taking a wholistic approach to humanity as opposed to a focus on divided gender stereotypes.

This leaves us with the question, what are the characteristics for the 21st century man? What does conscious masculinity look like? But before reading any further, I do hope you'll do the following activity.

Activity 7: Cpt 17—Characteristics for the 21st Century Man

Make a note of what you think the characteristics should be for the 21st century man.

If you are a 21st century man, to what extent do you possess those characteristics already?

For those men who don't possess those characteristics, how hard do you think it would be to change?

It's at this point that I must invoke the words of the ancient Greek philosopher, Socrates. "All I know is that I don't have all the answers, but I believe in the value of cooperative, rational, deliberative discussion".

And so to start the discussion I suggest the following.

The so-called negative masculine traits don't need to be abandoned completely, just tweaked. Here are some examples of what I mean.

POSITIVE MASCULINE TWEAKS

✓ control and domination →
    equality-based care and protection
✓ power-over → power-with
✓ aggression → assertion
✓ competition → cooperation
✓ List other tweaks that you can think of

The characteristics of control and domination need to be transformed to those of equality-based care and protection. Power-over needs to be transformed to power-with. Changing aggression to assertion will emerge in an appropriate way with the adoption of the ethical virtue of selfless self-love. And most definitely the need to compete must be transformed to one of cooperation.

Not that I'm suggesting an end to all forms of competition, but as Lao-Tzu said when talking about ego and leadership: "Leaders still love to compete, but they do it in the spirit of play".

There is no longer a need to "compete" for a mate unless you're on the TV show, *The Bachelorette*. The negative zero-sum results of competition are often death in some form — physical or metaphorical. Traits like individuality and independence still have a role when combined with humility. And self-centred ambition needs to have the self-centred part removed.

The so-called more positive traits like analytical and concrete thinking, logic, reason, and mathematics are still important and positive, but need to be done from a wholistic systemic perspective [see *Conscious Intelligence Competencies* — Step 4].

Societal attitudes in general also need to make some major changes. As an example, just as more and more countries are embracing same-sex marriage, we must be open to the idea of men being stay-at-home dads if that suits the family structure better.

In Appendix B, I speak about stay-at-home dads with the wonderful example of the very progressive Prime Minister of New Zealand, Jacinda Ardern, whose life-partner is a stay-at-home dad — and why shouldn't he be? He stays home and takes care of their baby while she goes out each day and takes care of the country – how fantastic is that!

If as a society we want to have equality, and have women paid the same salary as men for the same work, and be permitted to do the same jobs as men if they're able; then we as a society must learn to accept those role reversals in all areas. It's called "equality"!

In addition, men and women alike need to habituate all the loving virtuous actions that our specific life requires to make us the best possible "conscious" human we can become. And once men tweak and so transform those current-day negative masculine traits, then the habituation of the loving virtuous traits will be easy to acquire.

And finally, it's most important that we, as a society, encourage and praise men for demonstrating those loving virtuous actions including openness, vulnerability, selfless self-love, and self-control.

So again, where to start?

Activity 8: Cpt 17—Finding a Balance

Set up a list that you can keep adding to over the coming days, weeks, months, of what a male/female balance in society would be like.

1. Give some examples of what that balance would be like in your home, in your community, and in your workplace?

2. Does that balance already exist in your home, community, workplace? If so, in what way? If not, why not?

~ Chapter 18 ~
Steps for Positive Change

Only a few find the way, some don't recognize it when
they do – some… don't ever want to.

~ The Cheshire Cat ~
Alice in Wonderland

O nce again, I begin this chapter by invoking the words of Socrates. "All I know is that I don't have all the answers, but I believe in the value of cooperative, rational, deliberative discussion".

So having presented evidence of the rise of positive feminine-energy and the death-throes of negative-masculine-energy, many men might feel as if their lives no longer have meaning because they have to let go of their deep-seated, inherent, evolutionary "power-over" others. This might leave them feeling as if there's a void or a vacuum in their lives. And as Aristotle taught us, "Nature Abhors a Vacuum". And that vacuum will be filled with whatever comes along, which could be either positive or negative.

To prevent that vacuum being filled with negative attitudes and actions, instead of men being condemned, as so many newly empowered egocentric women are doing, men need to be supported. A perfect role for *conscious* feminists.

The woods were dark and foreboding, and Alice sensed that sinister eyes were watching her every step. Worst of all, she knew that Nature abhorred a vacuum.

The Far Side ~ Gary Larson

Ideally partnering with appropriate positive-energy women to learn these new virtuous 2 characteristics will assist men to understand what this new time of positive feminine-energy is all about and how to integrate it into their lives. This will ensure that their obsolete negative masculine-energy eventually gets overwritten.

To that end, some time ago I suggested that it was time for a *Transformational* Men's Movement — 21st Century Style.

A *Transformational* **Men's Movement**

While the time was certainly right for the #MeToo Movement, we also need a *Transformational* Men's Movement to fill the void created by the end of negative masculine-energy.

Even though a so-called "Men's Movement" emerged in many Western countries in the 1960s and 1970s, it included such things as "Men's Rights" and "Men's Liberation", neither of which are necessarily open to adopting the conscious characteristics of the new rising feminine-*energy*.

While the underpinning aim of the various Men's Movements was generally one of self-improvement, the focus of these improvements covered many different areas.

And past Men's Movements or not, the first thing currently filling any current vacuum is confusion which, ever since the #MeToo Movement, I'm hearing and seeing across all communities every day.

More than likely many men will feel, erroneously albeit understandably, threatened either on a conscious or non-conscious level, by this new surge of feminine-energy with all the do's and don'ts of the #MeToo Movement. These threatening feelings could well lead men to react in the only way all too many men have been taught — with even more negative masculine actions of domination, control. And concerningly, this could lead to an escalation of anti-social acts, especially domestic violence of all kinds.

While those negative reactions might be instinctive reactions, I'm in no way condoning any of those actions or saying that being instinctive can be offered as an excuse. They cannot and must not.

I'm just highlighting some of the potential unintended negative consequences that have clearly not been considered by women calling for violence against men.

But it should be noted that the out-dated 1000 millennium abusive actions of these men will no longer be supported by the new 2000 millennium rising global feminine-energy, which will lead to even greater confusion for men.

Indeed, the more controlling men become, the more the new 2 energy will reject those actions, and so the more likely it will be that those men will lose all the relationships they're trying so desperately to cling on to with their controlling actions. These lost relationships could include their partner, their family, even social and work relationships.

So there's an urgent need to start a new unified men's movement, identified by the addition of the word transformational — the *Transformational* Men's Movement — because it's the men on this planet today who'll have to make the greatest conscious transformations.

Women and our beautiful Gen Zs are more likely to inherently adopt the new feminine-energy characteristics. But many men will need to learn these new ways of living, acting, and being in our new world. And when they do, they'll then experience so many mental and physical health benefits.

Not only that but they'll also experience far more successful loving relationships in all areas of their lives, which in turn will also lead to greater success in all areas of their new "loving world".

However, many men will find it very difficult to accept these inevitable changes. But if they do accept the changes and then instead of focusing on what they're losing, focus on developing their exciting new life ahead, they'll have a new purpose in life — to live the very best love-in-action life of conscious masculinity they possibly can.

As I often say, there's no greater source of happiness, well-being, health, and longevity than to have a life filled with meaning and purpose.

So again, where to start?

First Two Steps

(1) The very first transformational step must be to acknowledge and accept that the world has changed and what might have been a necessary trait once, no longer applies. Any man who's not prepared to acknowledge and accept those changes might as well toss in the towel now and brace for the consequences of an unhappy and unfulfilled life going forward.

(2) Next is to acknowledge and accept that in this 21st century, physical size and physical strength does not equate to superiority. And just because a man is a man, that doesn't mean that they are superior to women in any way at all.

They might be different to women in many ways, but not superior, which by definition means that women are not inferior creatures. And when both men and society can accept that women are not inferior, men are more likely to be open to adopting the characteristics of positive feminine-energy that were previously thought to be weak and inferior.

Similarly, even in this world of rising feminine-energy, women are not to be regarded as being superior to men. The key as always is an attitude of equality.

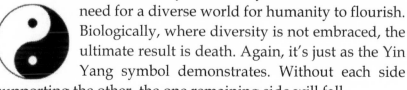 I often talk about unity in diversity and the fundamental need for a diverse world for humanity to flourish. Biologically, where diversity is not embraced, the ultimate result is death. Again, it's just as the Yin Yang symbol demonstrates. Without each side supporting the other, the one remaining side will fall.

Now with an acceptance of those two foundational steps, it's essential for men to continually work on enhancing the first three Conscious Intelligence Competencies — (1) Self-Awareness; (2) Self-Love and Self Compassion; and (3) Self-Control. And you can find out how to do that in *Conscious Self-Discovery: Enriching Your Relationship with Yourself.*

Filling the Void

The process of positive transformation will be a lot easier for men if they're supported by at least two of the following.

I. Those Who Care About Them

Most people have some others in their lives who care about them, be it a family member or a close friend. These are the people who can be of great support to someone going through any sort of transformational change.

Nevertheless, there are all too many people who, for whatever reason, have no family to turn to. And even close understanding and so supportive friends are non-existent. These are the people who really need to find other men going through the same changes, no matter how much of a hermit they might think they prefer to be.

2. Other Men Going Through the Same Process

There's no better way for men to network with each other and support each other than through a new, global Men's Movement.

This new Men's Movement should not be about a slow *evolution.* The time is now for men to learn how to *transform* as rapidly as possible to live in harmony with the way the 21st century requires. Again, this new Men's Movement needs to be a **_Transformational_** Men's Movement.

The partnership and support offered by such a movement needs to be 100% aligned with our new conscious, feminine-2-energy values and traits, such as partnership, support, and cooperation.

And equally important, it's essential that men focus on all the positive reasons for gaining those new traits, as opposed to focusing on what they might think they're losing. And when they do focus on what they're gaining, men will be given a sense of meaning and purpose as they strive to achieve the most conscious changes they possible can in our new world.

3. Society as a Whole

One of the first ways to get society to accept these transformative changes in men is to get the media and entertainment industry on board. And with this in mind, let me share an anecdotal story of how powerful the media can be in these cases.

As I've mentioned I'm the survivor of what was primarily a very psychologically abusive marriage. Also like all too many survivors of marital psychological abuse, I also experienced childhood psychological abuse.

And as you'll recall me saying, it's very common for people who've been psychologically abused as children to go on and be psychologically abused as adults and not even realise what is being done to them. And why should they? As a child they were brought up to believe that's how they were meant to be treated by the people they loved. So they felt at home in that psychologically abusive adult environment.

And that was certainly my story. Like all too many people, in those days I too thought domestic violence was just about bruises, broken bones, and/or sexual assault.

However in the early 1980s, some years after escaping what I was later to discover was a very abusive marriage, I was watching the television soapy, *The Young and the Restless*. At that time *The Young and the Restless* used to have ongoing episodes focusing on various social issues. Maybe they still do. I haven't seen the show in decades. But in Australia in the early 1980s, *The Young and the Restless* ran a series of episodes on domestic violence. Australia was always many years behind what was screened in the States.

In this series on domestic violence, lawyer Cricket Blair was working with various domestic violence victims. The various victim/survivors of psychological abuse told Cricket about the things their husbands had done or said to them.

Day after day as I watched each episode all those years ago, I was wide-eyed and shocked at what I was learning. I kept saying to the screen—"that's what my husband did to me", "yes, I know exactly how that feels, that's what happened to me".

It didn't take long before I realised that even though I had no bruises or broken bones to show for it, I was indeed the survivor of very extreme domestic violence in the form of psychological abuse.

Sure, there were also the very negative physically "abusive" events in which I nearly lost my life. But it was his continuous psychological abuse or negative brainwashing if you like, that had taken hold and so he could have done anything to me—and did.

Nevertheless, even though for me it was well after the event, I was so grateful to those responsible for that *Young and the Restless* story-line because it really did change my life.

Such is the power of the media.

Similarly, when you see someone in a movie or on a TV show drinking a can of Coca Cola, or using an Apple laptop computer, that didn't happen just by chance because they were the only product-brands in the prop's cupboard at the time. It's called "product placement" and companies pay a fortune for it.

Such is the power of the media.

Just look at the societal acceptance of non-binary people leading to an ever-growing number of countries legalising same-sex marriage. Surely same-sex storylines on the screen with TV shows like "Modern Family" have had a great influence on those attitudinal changes; just as storylines of female US Presidents have at least opened the door for the right candidate there too.

Such is the power of the media.

The time really is now, especially after the #MeToo focus on Hollywood, for the media and entertainment industry to get on board. It's time they started producing movies and TV series demonstrating all the many benefits, and especially societal acceptability, of men transforming and subsequently acting in a more positive conscious form of masculinity. And I'm not talking about more homosexual or non-binary storylines.

It's important that they're based on typical heterosexual men moving to a more positive form of masculinity — Conscious Masculinity. James Bond ~ 21st Century Style would be a perfect example.

James Bond ~ 21ˢᵗ Century Style

I frequently hear people say that the next James Bond movie should be a *Jane* Bond film instead, with a "kick-arse" woman in the lead. But that's definitely NOT the change we need. We certainly don't want yet another woman trying to be like a "kick-arse" man, demonstrating outdated stereo-typical negative masculine-energy characteristics.

We need the next James Bond movie to star the same seemingly rugged good-looking "macho" James Bond but with "macho" being demonstrated in a brand-new way.

The storyline would still be of how 007 is able to "save the world" but from the perspective of using virtuous feminine-*energy* traits.

So the movie would have a backstory of how 007 saw that the world had changed and things had to be done differently, with men acting in a more peaceful collaborative manner using brains instead of brawn.

The backstory would demonstrate how he went about adopting these new ethical feminine-*energy* character traits. And then how he was able to make a <u>real</u> difference to the world using those softer, cooperative, ethically "loving" conscious, We not Me, characteristics.

It would be social change through Social Constructionism at its very best: "When people talk to each other the world gets constructed" — or re-constructed.

A Positive Feminine-Energy "Fortnite"

With that in mind, I'd like to propose one more way the entertainment industry could get on board.

Currently the world, especially the young teenage world, is consumed with the video game Fortnite in which weapons are gathered up to slay your opponents and survive to be the last living competitor. According to a Fortnite blog post, in less than a year after its launch, Fortnite grew to **125 *million*** players.

During a radio interview, a young 13-year-old boy was asked why he loved the game so much. Many of the features that attracted him were very positive such as the game's creativity; the complexity of the levels; the game's required strategies were constantly being changed and so challenging the player; and that it was a very social game where he was able to "hang out with his mates".

Also, apparently the characters do lots of different ritualised dances that players learn and do in real-life at school and on the footy field with their real-life mates. All great stuff.

However, the lad got really excited when asked what he found most addictive about Fortnite. He said "the satisfaction of the kill".

Later in the interview it was clear that he couldn't understand what was so wrong, or so negative and so violent about the thrill of the kill.

Fortnite is clearly still having a major impact throughout the world. So just imagine if a video game similar to Fortnite was developed with all of those very positive features, but instead of the thrill of the kill, the aim was some form of positive save-the-world goal where the heroes were both women and men. But the men were experiencing an incredibly exciting power of winning through the most co-operative, and peaceful, and "loving" actions—demonstrating the greatest positive feminine-2-*energetic* attributes. Perhaps Conscious Winning.

This would be a new form of very manly macho men that women loved. Points could be given for how many loving actions/moral virtues were used to achieve their goals instead of how many people they killed; with points being deducted for negative or violent actions. A creative video game like that could indeed change the world.

"When people talk together [play video-games together], the world gets constructed"– or re-constructed in either negative or positive ways. The choice is ours to make.

CAVEAT: Having just argued a case for developing a video game with a positive message, in no way do I abandon anything I've ever said about the very evil and negative side to video games (See *Conscious Self-Discovery*). In general, I still think they're insidiously evil and should be banned, especially due to the addictive nature purposely built into them. Like an abusive spouse, they brainwash the players. But if they are going to exist then at least give them a positive life affirming message. And maybe even a subtle message encouraging the player to stop gaming.

The Good, the Bad, and the Ugly

Since publishing the original parts of this book in 2017, the speed with which social changes are occurring around the world has gone into overdrive. These changes represent the good, the bad, and the very ugly. And I'd like to include just two relatively recent changes.

So let's start with the Bad that's very Ugly indeed and get it out of the way.

The Incel Movement—The Bad that's Very Ugly

Until April, 2018, I'd never heard of the Incel Movement. Incel stands for Involuntary Celibate. The movement was brought to light when 25-year-old, Alek Manassian, drove a van into a group of people in Toronto, Canada, on April 24th, 2018, and killed ten people and injured another sixteen.

I don't intend to say much about this here because I find the entire ideology behind the Incel Movement that allegedly inspired Manassian's actions to be sickening, repugnant, and down-right terrifying.

Some people say Incel is linked to a radicalised "Men's Rights" attitude, which is why I advocate a "*Transformational* Men's Movement" and not just a Men's Rights Movement at this time. And of course Incel, which has been around for several years now, has been able to grow exponentially due to social media.

My only reason for mentioning it is because it directly links to my comment in the previous chapter when I said: "Concerningly, this [rise of feminine-energy] could lead to an escalation of anti-social acts especially domestic violence of all kinds." And here we go.

Briefly, the Incel movement is a mainly male organisation whose members believe they are ***entitled*** to have a sexual relationship with a woman. And so they promote extremely misogynistic and violent views because they're not having the sexual relationships they want. These misogynistic and violent views are now turning into violent actions.

Now sure the world is filled with lonely people, but not violent, hate-filled people who believe they are entitled to have what they're not getting. Talk about *Me not We*.

In 2019, author and journalist, Clementine Ford[27], published a book called *Boys will be Boys* in which she documents Incel and similar attitudes. She says that these men have a "sense that women are people who are withholding from them the love and affection they feel they not only deserve but that defines them as men."

Those sorts of attitudes are at the extreme end of negative masculine-energy and need to be urgently addressed.

No doubt if these men changed their attitude to one of genuine love-in-action/ethics-in-action they just might find the love and relationships they long for.

The "MenCare" Program in Rwanda—the Good

When I was a little girl if I ever had to take any liquid medicine, mainly when I had a sore throat, once I'd swallowed the nasty tasting liquid I'd be given a piece of chocolate to remove the bad taste in my mouth. Well this next story is our much-needed piece of chocolate after hearing about the Incel Movement.

Early in 2015[28], 1199 men were recruited in various regions of Rwanda to participate in a randomised controlled trial to assess the effectiveness of what's been referred to as a MenCare Program. The program included couples' intervention, a gender-transformative program for men and couples to promote men's engagement in reproductive and maternal health, caregiving, and healthier couple relations. And the results have been wonderful and include:

❖ Reductions in men's dominance in household decision-making and improvements in the household division of labour.

❖ Greater contraceptive use.

❖ A significant reduction in the likelihood of both physical and sexual violence from a partner, as reported by women.

❖ Lower rates of violence against children.

I really love the label "MenCare" as it's not about everyone caring for men, but is about teaching men how to care for others — *We not Me* — beautiful, conscious feminine-energy in action.

These results certainly show what could be possible if a *Transformational Men's Movement* was implemented globally. Something we urgently need.

~ Chapter 19 ~
COVID-19 ~ Our Practice Run?

Nearly 40 years ago, in my "Power of Two" paper, I said that from 2020 on, we'd begin to live in a totally different world. Although I never guessed it would be heralded by a global pandemic.

~ Kashonia Carnegie ~

Sadly, after all the headway made by groups like Extinction Rebellion, and Greta Thunberg, for most people the immediate concerns about coronavirus make any worries about climate change look totally insignificant.

But it's not! It's about short-term versus long-term thinking.

Despite the catastrophic long-term results of ignoring our environmental issues, they are just that—*long-term issues.*

And so today, sure Australia might have been on fire and sure the climate is changing. But hey, you could get coronavirus tomorrow and die. Short-term versus long-term!

What will receive your greatest attention?

You'll recall that Step 7 in the Conscious Intelligence Competency Framework is, in part, about dig, dig, digging, way past any superficial assumptions no matter what the situation. So it's time to dig, dig, dig some more!

Nearly 40 years ago, in my "Power of Two" paper, I said that from 2020 on, we'd begin to live in a totally different world. And we will be, and most commentators agree.

A recent survey indicated that 65% of people said that COVID was the reset the world needs. And 58% want a simpler life. However, at this time every country is experiencing daily COVID deaths and infections and an unprecedented economic recession or worse.

Activity 9: Cpt 19—Changes You See

Make a list of some of the significant changes to the way we do things that you can see resulting from this   new COVID time. And will they be positive or negative changes? A little later in this chapter I have mentioned many changes that have come to my mind.

And so once again I invite you to get your shovel out and start digging, beginning with this next thought.

While conspiracy theories abound on social media about the source of the coronavirus, most scientists agree that it began with the human consumption of native animals being kept alive and sold in despicable and unethical wildlife wet markets in China. And there's a lot more to the story at that level too that I go into in *Conscious Environmental Sustainability* that will be out by the end of 2020.

Meanwhile however, just to give you something to think about regarding the source of this shocking pandemic. And again,

Transparency Time, because this is an area of one of my greatest passions.

In earlier chapters you read about the high school students taking to the streets saying enough is enough with respect to gun laws — or lack of them. Indeed I dubbed 2019 the year of protests with people saying enough is enough regarding all manner of issues.

In 2020, is COVID nature's way of saying enough is enough?

In one of my environmental tutorials, when I was a post-graduate university student, we had a long discussion about how smart humans *thought* they were.

We talked about how humans always considered themselves at the top of the food chain able to kill anything from mice to big elephants. But the one thing that was superior to humans was an unseen virus or bacteria that can kill us all. And now we're actually seeing that play out with COVID.

Before the industrialisation of agriculture, pandemics like COVID were rare. Sure there was the Black Death in the 14th century and the Spanish Flu after World War I. But in the last fifty years there's been an explosion of deadly pandemics in various parts of the world.

I'm sure you heard about them on the news, or some might have even affected where you live. You're no doubt familiar with names like Ebola, HIV, Swine Flu, Hendra Virus, Avian Flu, Zika Virus, SARS, West Nile Virus and on they go. And setting aside the loss of life, they have cost the world a financial fortune.

In the last ten years epidemiologists have "discovered" around 1000 of these "new" diseases just waiting to detonate on parts of the world, or globally as in the case of COVID.

Why? You might well ask — and I hope you do.

The general thought amongst scientists is that it's because of the destruction of our natural world, and the major ever-growing loss of species and biodiversity.

As I've written many times in many different books, the result of a lack of diversity in all things is death, in one form or another. Yet we've cleared over 40% of the Earth's surface just to feed and graze livestock so people can continue to eat meat. Yet it's vegetarians that have the bad name! And yes, I am a vegetarian.

Many environmentalists blame overpopulation for many of our environmental woes. But that is only part of the problem. Again, dig, dig, dig, and you'll find that it's the *way* we humans choose to live with capitalism in control, instead of allowing the natural cycle of things to play out.

Just like climate change has been put on the back burner for far too long, we humans refuse to contemplate, let alone discuss what we've done, and are doing, to our natural cycle of life. We're too focused on *Me not We.* And "we" must always include our non-human world too.

So let's keep digging while we wait for the next global pandemic.

In Chapter 10, I posed the following questions that I originally asked in a 2017 publication. "The next global financial crisis could occur at any time. And when it does, (1) will it also be born of an unethical negative masculine-energy and arrogance at play? And (2) will it finally herald the last breath of negative masculine-energy and the final turning point to our new world? We'll see".

Well we didn't have to wait very long to see. The "next global financial crisis" is now here with the arrival of COVID-19.

For years I've been saying that that next global financial crisis would make the 2007-2009 Global Financial Crisis (The

Great Recession) look like a walk in the park. And with lockdowns, walking in the park is now a problem.

It's true that there's a big difference between this recession and the 2007-2009 recession.

The 2007-2009 recession was generally known as a Supply Shock Recession where people didn't have the money to pay for their escalating mortgages and other goods. In other words businesses were open and wanting to sell their goods and services but people had no money to buy anything.

By contrast, this COVID-led recession is what has sometimes been called a Demand Shock recession. Because while it's true that a great many people have lost their job and so have no spare money to spend. But that is only because so many businesses have been forced to close due to the Virus, and people are in lockdown. So no one is able to go out and buy the goods that they would normally go out and buy. As a result, the economy is affected by the lack of demand.

But we still need to dig, dig, dig farther.

And I suggest that both climate change and the global pandemic that has caused the current/forthcoming recession, have the self-same deeper source. That common source is leading us to live in an unsustainable and so unethical *me not we* way. The source is our out-dated and totally unsustainable global form of economics—neo-classical capitalism and the growth economy, and the associated power of the so-called "elites" and the erroneously-named political "strongmen".

Everything is Linked to Everything Else
(Step 4 in the Conscious Intelligence Competency Framework)

While the virus might have started in the wildlife wet markets, scientists globally tell us that if we'd known about the outbreak when it first erupted, in late 2019, the world would be a different place today.

So I invite you to grab your own shovel and reflect on some of the following questions. And as you dig, keep in mind all that I've been saying about our outdated capitalistic growth economy, the power of the "elites", and so-called political "strongmen" — all born of **Me not We** negative masculine-energy or the attitudes, mindsets, and their resulting actions. And see if any of that shows up in these questions.

❖ Why wasn't the world warned about the virus in 2019?

❖ Why did the leaders of so many countries dismiss the virus as a passing non-issue when it was first given global exposure and the scientists loudly warned of the impending doom?

❖ Who were the leaders of the countries that dismissed the virus versus those who immediately took it seriously?

❖ Why is the wildlife section of the Asian wet markets allowed to continue when there have been so many calls over the years for it to be shut down due to animal rights, human health, and environmental reasons?

❖ Are these heart-breaking wild animals necessary to feed the poor, or purely available as a misguided delicacy for the rich to buy?

❖ Why were the owners/operators of the luxury cruise-ships reluctant to take timely action, but instead let their vessels become what became known as floating Petri dishes.

❖ And a question only you can answer. Which is more important; human health or continuing to grow the economy, keeping in mind that our current system of economics was never intended to be anything more than a temporary measure. Yet here we are almost 100 years later thinking it's the only game in town[29]. With an economic system in harmony with our 21st century, maybe we could have had both, healthy humans and a healthy economy.

So just keep dig, dig, digging and reflecting.

A Conscious Economy

It's only with ethical sustainability that our earth and our society can flourish. And ethical sustainability teaches us that the environmental, the social, and the economic are all inter-related. They each impact on each other.

Everything is Linked to Everything Else

So before looking into the social impacts, both positive and negative, of COVID-19, I'd like to get the economic side out of the way

And before we start digging into a conscious economy permit me to explain why I'm including this section at all. And by the way, the second half of this chapter is a lot happier, lighter, and more fun.

Meanwhile, the only way to come through the great economic costs of the COVID recession in a socially just manner is to look to a major "conscious change today" from our current out-dated *Me not We* economic system to a Conscious *Me to We* Economy—Conscious Economic Sustainability.

A Conscious Economy, by definition, is all about a totally different *we not me* system of economics. And the more people who even have a very basic awareness of what it could be like, the more likely it is for conscious change like this to occur.

As Bernie Sanders says, change always comes from the bottom up—from you and me.

Philosopher David Hume was another who said, in essence, that ultimate power comes from the people.

Now I admit for some people there will be elements of this Conscious Economy section when their eyes might glaze over. And if that does happen to you, then just skim over the next few pages. It's amazing what your non-conscious mind will pick up even if you just do that.

So with a large percentage of people actually excited about what our Post-COVID world might look like, hoping for the "reset the world needed", surely there can be no better time for a brand new global Conscious Economy.

Not only do we need a new system of economics to recover from the COVID-recession, but the global aging population, and climate change, are also unavoidable major economic threats currently knocking very loudly on our door.

And when I talk about a brand-new Conscious Economy, I'm not just talking about a few tweaks here and there. I mean a genuine second-order change, which is when we move from one system to a totally different system.

In other words, we no longer move the deck-chairs on the Titanic—that's a first-order change which never works. We'll still drown.

As Einstein said: "We cannot solve our problems with the same level of thinking that created them".

Instead we remove the rope from each deck-chair on the Titanic and use that rope to tie bundles of deck-chairs together to form a whole mob of rafts. We then throw the rafts into the *ocean*, which is a totally different *system* to the system called the ship Titanic. We can then float away to safety on our deck-chair rafts. So second-order change is about leaving the old dysfunctional system (the Titanic) and moving in to a brand-new system (the ocean) and starting life afresh again.

Before giving any thought to a second-order change to our economic system, here are two quotes that are worth keeping in mind. They come from John Maynard Keynes, considered the founder of modern macroeconomics.

"Capitalism is the astounding *belief* that the most wicked of men will do the most wicked of things for the greatest good of everyone".[30]

And then in 1933 Keynes[31] also wrote:

The decadent international but individualistic capitalism, in the hands of which we found ourselves after the War, is not a success. It is not intelligent, it is not beautiful, it is not just, it is not virtuous — and it does not deliver the goods. In short, we dislike it and we are beginning to despise it.

Why is it that we've advanced in so many areas in the last close to 100 years, but not economically?

Where would we be today if we were still driving the same cars as were around 100 years ago? Or flying in the same 100-year-old aeroplanes? Or coping with 100-year-old communication systems? I'll let you add to the list.

So why are we so desperate to cling to an out-dated economic system that is the source of such great global inequality.

The pandemic has led to a couple of interesting organisations such as Millionaires for Humanity and Millionaires against Pitchforks. Both of these groups have written open letters, signed by several hundred multi-millionaires from many different countries, all begging their governments to increase their level of income tax to help cover COVID expenses.

These groups are not to be confused with The Giving Pledge Movement that was formed by forty billionaires in 2010.

The Giving Pledge is a movement of philanthropists who commit to giving the majority of their wealth to philanthropy or charitable causes, either during their lifetimes or in their wills. Today there are now 210 members, from 23 countries, ranging in ages from 30-90 years of age.

While the billionaires' group are philanthropists choosing the groups and charities they will donate to, the two Millionaires' groups are calling for their respective government to take more of their income. There are pluses and minuses with both models that I look at in *Conscious Economic Sustainability: Equality and an Ethically Sustainable Financial System in Our Post-COVID World* (due out late-2020).

However, instead of doing what the millionaires say should be done, and increase their taxes, most Western countries are doing the opposite ASAP? They're cutting taxes based on the outdated and erroneous belief in the 18th Century trickle-down effect. This is the belief that if the government takes care of the rich, the rich will give jobs to the poor. Now that might have been the case in the mid-1700s when Adam Smith suggested such an idea. But that 250-year-old concept does not happen in our current world.

The only people/organisation that can **guarantee** jobs to the unemployed is the government itself.

The other reason often given for governments cutting taxes is the belief that if someone pays less tax, they will have more money in their wallet that they can then spend to help stimulate growth, and so help the economy.

The problem with that belief is that the greatest beneficiaries of lower taxes are normally the very rich. And the very rich will not spend more money just because they're paying lower taxes. They have enough money to buy whatever they want, whenever they want it, with or without the lower taxes.

The only people to immediately spend any extra money that comes their way through tax cuts or government benefits are the poor. Yet they are not earning enough, if anything at all, for the tax cuts to make much difference to them or the economy.

In *Conscious Economic Sustainability*, I go into the state of our current neo-classical economic world in a very basic down-to earth way and review a number of alternative models that have been presented over time. But there are two models that I really focus on: (1) An Economy for the Common Good and (2) Modern Monetary Theory.

Ideally, as a Conscious Change/Sustainability Ethicist, I would love to see an amalgamation of those two models.

Now I won't even attempt to explain "An Economy for the Common Good" at this time, except to say it has some similarities to Bhutan's economic system based on Gross

National Happiness, instead of our outdated Gross National/Domestic Product.

However, in the past year or so, and especially since the arrival of the COVID recession and unemployment, Modern Monetary Theory—aka MMT—is being spoken about in glowing terms by more and more economists, in all corners of the globe, every day.

And interestingly, most of these economists say that initially they thought MMT was rubbish and would never work. And I must admit that I too was in that camp when I first heard MMT mentioned.

But after some dig, dig, digging with an open-mind many economists have been left seeing MMT as the economic change the world has been so desperately waiting for.

Again in *Conscious Economic Sustainability*, I discuss MMT at greater length. But very briefly, Professor Stephanie Kelton, former chief economist on the United States Senate Budget Committee and author of the New York Times best-seller, *The Deficit Myth: Modern Monetary Theory and How to Build a Better Economy*, defines MMT this way.

"MMT is about replacing an artificial financing constraint with an inflation constraint". In other words, in neo-classical economics this *"artificial* financing constraint" is the notion that the government should not spend more than it receives from taxes, trading, investments, and the like. If they do they'll have to "borrow" the money from somewhere and end up with a deficit, which is seen as very bad.

And I'll come to the "inflation constraint" part in a minute.

Professor Kelton explains that governments and media alike try to describe government spending to the public as being akin to someone's household budget. The government can't spend more than they earn or they'll have to get a loan from someone that will have to be repaid. And so the average Jo Public says okay, I certainly understand what that's all about.

But the truth is that in any country with a central banking sovereign-monetary system, it's the federal government that actually issues the money. There is nowhere else the money can come from. These are countries like the USA, UK, Australia, and Canada. So they never have to "borrow" the money from anywhere, in the same way that you or I, or countries like members of European Union (EU) without monetary sovereignty might have to do.

Interestingly, even when the UK was a member of the EU the one thing it insisted on doing was to retain its monetary sovereignty. The UK always had the pound or new pound, and never the Euro.

And this is where the critics of MMT come in. If the government just spend more than they have received from trade or where ever, the only way they can get more money is to print it—commonly known as "quantitative easing". I'm sure the term is familiar to you.

In attempting to explain to the public how bad quantitative easing is, the MMT critics again refer to people like you and me, and say if *we* print money we'll end up in jail—so it must be wrong.

Another argument they give against MMT is that if a country can just print more and more money, they'll keep spending more and more, and it will just lead to hyper-inflation and the country ends up in a disastrous collapse.

This is where we introduce the "inflation constraint" aspect of MMT. You'll recall the definition of MMT as being "about replacing an artificial financing constraint with an inflation constraint". The problem with countries that experience hyper-inflation is that they place no constraint of any kind on what they're doing.

MMT says we *must* have a constraint of some kind, it's just that we currently have the wrong constraint with financing constraint.

Again, financing constraint is about how much spending the government can do based on the money it's received from trade and taxes and the like.

By contrast, an inflation constraint is based how much money the nation's business world is making, and how many people have jobs, and so how much they are able to spend. And it is *very* closely monitored.

But, you might be saying, why worry about all of this? Surely it's all too confusing. And to a degree, I agree. The finer details are all best left to the MMT economists.

And maybe that is a good idea, because I recently heard a sociologist talking on radio criticizing MMT. He said it would take away from people all the human-dignity of having a job by just giving them a universal income — so a basic income without work. When the exact opposite is true with MMT.

So long as that inflation constraint is in place and monitored closely, MMT means that there can be virtually no unemployment or under-employment — *everyone* will have the human-dignity of a job.

This means that more money will be spent on goods and services due to full employment. And more money can be spent on environmental concerns and social issues like schools, hospitals, and social housing. And the more money spent on those social issues, the more money is actually going into the businesses providing those necessary goods and services.

Therefore, the more money circulating in the market place; the more the government will be able to spend on more social infrastructure; again ensuring everyone who wants a job will have a job. Not bad is it!

However, any major change to a social system tends to frighten many people, especially politicians who are scared that they won't be re-elected.

Yet for countries with monetary sovereignty, the bottom line is that MMT is good for the economy, it's good for the environment, it's good for the community, and it's good for business. And it's about time that a temporary economic system that's now nearly 100 years old was updated to suit our modern world, especially if it included elements of an "Economy for the Common Good".

Not only that, but MMT is probably the only economic system that won't see the young people of today paying off our COVID recession debt for the next 50 years.

"We're All in This Together"—Me to We

While you reflect on all that's happening at this time, 2020 can indeed be the start of a whole new *positive* way of life on our planet as the trending millennium numbers indicate.

Permit me to repeat the words of the ancient Greek, Phaedrus:

Things are not always what they seem; the first appearance deceives many; the intelligence of a few perceives what has been carefully hidden.

On a metaphysical/spiritual/quantum level, is it just possible that our current global chaos, with both COVID-19 and the global recession, is in fact a total global cleansing. A metaphoric cleansing in preparation for a brand-new start, born of a new way of thinking about our world and our global relationships?

Has that metaphoric boil that I keep mentioning actually just burst and the mess that has to be cleaned up is demonstrated by the aftermath of the coronavirus? And after that — the global chaotic pain is over and replaced by our new world?

We keep on hearing that after the virus has gone, life will never be the same. And I have absolutely no doubt that's 100% correct.

My mother was a young girl when the Spanish Flu hit the world after World War I. And until the day she died at the age of 93, she would frequently recount what it was like to live through the Spanish Flu. Such was the impact of that pandemic on her young life.

But on a more positive note, many years ago I was living in the Australian state of Queensland in an area known as the "food bowl" for the region.

It was a time of one of our many extreme droughts. Yet most of the farmers *irrigated* their crops, drought or no drought, and this was becoming harder and harder to do due to the lack of water.

And one of the greatest sources of water was being used by an orchardist to keep his fruit trees flourishing. Like his family before him, he continually used overhead sprinklers until he was ordered to stop using them because the water was just not available to him.

Now as I'm sure you'd be aware, a major problem in using overhead sprinklers to irrigate, or to water anything, is that the evaporation rate is enormous. So only a fraction of the water used does any good.

And now he'd been ordered to reduce his water consumption by about 90%. So using overhead sprinklers with the associated evaporation would not only have all his trees die, but the region would be without supplies of fruit. He was devastated and didn't know what he was going to do.

But as the old saying goes, desperate times call for desperate measures.

So after his initial period of distress, the orchardist devised an underground method of suppling an abundance of water to all his trees, consuming no more that the allocated 10% of his original usage.

Needless to say after the drought was over he continued to produce the best fruit around on just that 10% of water. In addition, he only had to pay 10% of the price he used to pay for water. So he made more money while producing a better-quality fruit, and the community was left with more available water supplies for others to use—*We not Me* or Win/ Win/ Win!

But why did it have to take a desperate time to come up with such a sustainable idea? But it did.

Life is never the same after a disaster.

And if ever times were desperate, it's now. So like the orchardist, it's about turning those proverbial coronavirus lemons into loving conscious-based lemonade.

As an example, is it possible that those who've lost their job due to COVID shut-downs could now decide that it's time to start an entirely new career, or even some form of self-employment?

So at an "opportune" time like this, if you are currently out of work, are you going to sit down and complain about the world and your situation? Or will you actually take advantage of the lockdown, when you might well be getting some sort of government stipend, and get excited about what's ahead and do something to really make a difference to your own life and maybe even the lives of others?

Post-Corona Business Opportunities

At least two very distinct business opportunities are waiting for those who want to pursue them in our post-COVID world. And there is no better time than during the lockdown to do the research and start preparing.

Hands-On Industry

For those who like physical hands-on work the sky's the limit.

Currently, people everywhere are replacing flower beds in their garden with vegetable patches, for obvious reasons. And as an aside, nothing tastes better than fresh home-grown organic vegetables. So in our post-COVID world there has to be the need for people to maintain those vegie gardens, or even go door-to-door offering to set-up new ones for an appropriate fee.

If you're the hands-on type, maybe you could take up work as a handy-person. Or you could make some jewellery, or craft work, or raincoats for dogs, so that when this is all over you have some goods in stock to open a stall at the local market.

What do you enjoy doing as a hobby? Surely it's possible that if you enjoy doing these things, others might enjoy buying what you make to give as a gift.

One more thought before I move on. BC — Before COVID — what did your best mates ask you to help them with? PC — Post COVID — chances are that others without a best mate like you might just need to have that same sort of help and would be very happy to pay you for it.

Now to the greatest growth industry in the world today.

The Digital/Tech Economy

One of the first Internet entrepreneurs I ever heard about was a man who lived in our Outback, Northern Territory region. I'm sure it would have been in the 1990s. He made leather stock-whips, and leather belts, and the like.

It was something he enjoyed doing and he was able to eke out a meagre living doing it. Then the Internet arrived and he decided to sell his products on line and he made a fortune, and probably still does.

So if you don't like the idea of selling raincoats for dogs to locals at the market — sell them on line to the world.

But a word of warning. Don't expect to become an overnight millionaire. And if anyone says they'll teach you how to become an overnight millionaire — just remember "social-distancing". They are the people to avoid like the virus.

Nevertheless, start selling something, anything, on line and you'll never lose your job again if there's another global lockdown. There'll always be people somewhere in the world with money.

Not surprisingly, one of the biggest Internet markets is the "learning industry".

And you don't need an alphabet soup after your name to teach others something that you're good at. We're all good at something.

So what do you enjoy doing, that you could teach others about? What hardships have you been through and yet come out the other side? Teach people how you did that. As someone said: "Turn your Mess into a Message!"

I keep hearing about so many people, at this time, who used to run live classes teaching yoga, exercise, dance, cooking, you name it. And due to the lockdown, they now run their classes on You Tube or TikTok.

And guess what? Instead of having just 10 or 20 people in their class, they're now getting 10 or 20 THOUSAND!

What a new business opportunity they now have. An opportunity they never would have developed had it not been for the lockdowns.

So again, what do people want or need that you enjoy doing or know something about? Go and use this lockdown time to prepare for a whole new way of life.

Remember, at this time we most need supermarket and health care workers. Not hedge-fund managers.

This need not be a negative time at all, but the start of something really wonderful and exciting. The Choice is Yours; The Time is Now; It's Up to You.

Activity 10: Cpt 19—What Business Opportunity is Waiting for YOU

Before moving on, just stop for a moment and make a few lists that you can keep adding to.
1. List all the things that you enjoy doing.
2. List your greatest passions.
3. List all the skills you have.
4. List all the life-lessons you've had.
5. List all the times you've helped a mate – what did you do?
6. Now go through all those different lists and highlight any that you think you might enjoy being PAID to do, or any that you could teach others how to do.

1st Wave versus 2nd Wave

In mid-March 2020 when most countries went into lockdown, the world changed because everyone throughout most of the world were having the same, never-before, experiences.

And then, mainly because of the great economic concerns, political leaders began opening up the economy as soon as they could despite the advice being given to them by the health professionals. The result for many areas was that a second COVID wave hit, as predicted by most of the health professionals.

The result of the 2nd wave is that just when the community thought the virus would be gone and life as normal would return, they've had to go back into any one of a number of forms of lockdown and quarantine. And because those second lockdowns were not as universal, or as novel, as was the 1st wave, the public reaction has been somewhat different.

With the first wave lockdowns, for many, it was almost a party-like atmosphere. By contrast, the second wave has had a darker more depressed sensation and brought resignation from some, and denial, and rebelliousness, and anger from others. There seems to be a greater sense of community fear that this virus is either back or unable to be controlled. And with the fear is a sense of not knowing what to expect next and when will it ever end.

Even so, many of the same beautiful, #2 forms of conscious acts of kindness can still be found under the surface in many areas, even though they are certainly not publicised as much as they were during the 1st Wave.

However, short of a vaccine, we will have to learn to live with COVID to some degree for quite some time to come. Will that mean a continual game of Whac-A-Mole? Quite likely.

So for the record, I'd now like to review what happened during the first COVID wave. Because apart from those who suffered from actually getting the virus, or losing a loved one, the much-publicised actions in that first wave are worth repeating in subsequent lockdowns if they come your way.

Our New World of Loving Kindness— ### We not Me

During the first lockdown we all had to learn how to live a totally different lifestyle. A more caring lifestyle. A far simpler lifestyle, that again around 58% of people are calling for. A more family-oriented lifestyle—which can have its minuses as well as its pluses.

And apart from people fighting over toilet rolls, most people came together to help each other in some incredibly beautiful and creative ways.

Leaders were not only calling for more kindness and compassion towards others at that time, but people on all levels were automatically engaging in random acts of kindness, like checking on neighbours especially if they're elderly, taking leisurely walks around the block, or going camping with the kids in their own back yard.

In talking about the way the world came together to fix the Y2K threat of computers not clicking over to 2000; I said that it shows that *it is possible* for the world to come together as one if the will is there.

And that's exactly what happened during the 1st wave, and for many is now happening again. Here are just a few of the dozens and dozens of positive things that I kept hearing about with indications of possible post-COVID changes.

❖ People who never before worked from home are now doing that quite successfully, even radio broadcasters and TV talk-show hosts. So no commuter expense, or commuter stress and wasted hours. Not only that, but what a wonderful advantage for women with children to now know that they can indeed successfully work flexible hours from home— the power of two at work in **20**2**0** at its best.

❖ High-rise city office buildings might have to be converted into residential apartments because the need for massive office space will no longer be required.

❖ Workshops and meetings that once had people flying in from all over the world are still going ahead very successfully, but virtually, online in some form of video conferencing.

❖ Overall, the environment is thanking the coronavirus like never before. The global lockdowns resulted in a major reduction in the number of cars on the road and planes in the sky. The result is that throughout the world, the air we breathe is 20 – 50 times and in some cases 90 times cleaner than before. The constant smog over major landmarks has cleared. For instance, there's a 40% reduction in pollution over Beijing and the Great Wall of China. And the Himalayas can now be seen for the first time from 200 kilometres away. And the water in the canals in Venice is clean. If only we could learn from these examples.

❖ Perhaps there'll be a return to cloth nappies which are cheaper and better for the environment than all those massive packets of disposable nappies. And this then reopens up another former business opportunity of starting a pick-up nappy washing service.

❖ And talking of a return to a former industry. I know many people who say that they'll never go to another movie theatre, even when we no longer have to physically-distance. So maybe there's a great business opening for a return to Drive-In movies again.

❖ With gyms having to close off then on and off and on again, due to physical-distancing, there must be an increase in the sale of home-gym equipment.

❖ And will we ever go back to shaking hands?

❖ Parents who are having to home-school their children during the lockdown are gaining a whole new respect for the work of our often-maligned and abused teachers. Just as we're rightfully having new respect for the drivers of delivery vehicles — large and small; health care workers; supermarket workers; and so many other people who sadly meant very little to us in the past.

Cleaners are one such group. One cleaner was interviewed and asked what concerns you most about the work you're doing. His answer was: "Knowing that each time I enter a room, the Virus is in there, somewhere, with me". Makes you think, doesn't it!

❖ At the start of the 1st Wave, there was a coffee shop near an unemployment office where a queue of people almost a kilometre long had been waiting for hours and hours to register for unemployment benefits. And suddenly strangers — people just passing by — started to give money to the coffee shop so that the coffee shop could provide free cups of coffee to those who'd just lost their job due to the virus. How beautiful is that!

❖ Balcony "parties" were taking place the world over with residents in apartment blocks coming out onto their balcony singing to each other, and dancing or exercising together — but apart. Or they were coming out to give a united *yaaaa for the day* to all the incredible health-care workers, who like the teachers are also gaining a much over-due level of respect. *YAAAAAAAAAAAAA.*

So everyone is getting to know their neighbours like never before. And those balcony parties are a great example of the inaccuracy in the term with which we're all so familiar, "social-distancing". What we really need to do is engage in *physical*-distancing,   but definitely not *social*-distancing, which is so important to all humans.

❖ And of course so many entertainers are still doing what they do best to help us all feel better. They stream live videos of impromptu performances.

❖ One of my favourite activities, and I'm not alone here, is the trend of placing a teddy bear of some kind in your front window or on your gate. This is so that when people go out for a walk around the streets, especially (but not only) if they have children with them, they can look for bears. This was all prompted by the Michael Rosen book, "We're Going on a Bear Hunt". And the tune that goes with that saying is a REAL earworm!

TRANSPARENCY TIME: I love Bears!!! So beware! Or should that be — Bear-Ware

❖ Everyday people are coming up with some of the most hilarious and creative ideas to put up on You Tube and TikTok. I thoroughly recommend this one called: "Quarantine day 7 — people getting bored". It's both hilarious and so very creative. There are a few with the same title but it's essential that you see this from the very beginning. So the full version video that runs for 42secs is at this URL

https://www.youtube.com/watch?v=ZKUpep0ozFM

What are you seeing here??????

The common call, "We're all in this together", and these random acts of kindness, compassion, caring about others, having fun, making each other laugh, living a simpler way of life, more family time, and the massive improvements to our natural environment are all **_exactly_** what living in harmony with the number **2** is all about.

*And of all times for the coronavirus to hit, resulting in all this loving behaviour—the start of 20**2**0. We've never had a date like that before! And never before have we been through what we're currently going through. And we've never shown such INSTINCTIVE loving kindness on a global level.*

Is "The Virus" nature's way of saying "enough is enough" it's time for a Global Change?

Activity 11: Cpt 19—Random Acts of Kindness—Simpler Life

While it's all still fresh in your mind, make a list, as long as possible, of all the funny, simpler, and beautiful things you've heard that people are doing during the coronavirus lockdowns.

Maybe these are things we can continue to do after all of the lockdowns are over.

Just as the rise in the status of women "coincidently" happened at this time — with the arrival of our new **2**000-millennium. Here we are at the very beginning of 2020 and sure the COVID situation has been forced on us, but again, amazingly what so many of us are instinctively doing during the pandemic is 100% in keeping with the characteristics  represented by that number 2-energy that the world is now focused on. Give it some thought.

Sure there are the toilet paper warriors — but those sorts of people will always be around.

But is it possible that when all this is coronavirus deal is over, like the orchardist, we'll have found a new way to live and work and interact with each other. If only we can continue to live that way we'll have a far more environmentally and economically sustainable world — something climate change so desperately needs.

Now it's true that humans are social creatures and there is something very special about sharing a meeting or workshop experience live with other humans. But after this is all over, perhaps we could continue to refrain from all the polluting air travel and satisfy our human need for live social interaction in even more special ways.

How do you think we might be able to do that?

You'll recall Oprah's words: "God [the universe] always whispers first". If we don't take any notice of the whisper the message will get stronger, and louder, and tougher, and more painful, until we finally take action.

At the moment COVID-19 is certainly making life pretty tough and painful. So from a different perspective, is COVID-19 how we're finally being *loudly and painfully* "told" by some metaphysical or quantum force that it is possible, and it is time, to begin living that more peaceful, loving, and sustainable life in harmony with the power of the 2 energy now in **20**2**0**, with its two 2s.

And sure by mid-202**1**, COVID could be just about over. But with the return of that masculine-1-energy, unfortunately it will be the masculine-energy that will start and rebuild what it lost in 2020 in the only way negative masculine-energy knows how.

But at least 2020 will have given us all a taste of what *is* possible in a conscious loving world of kindness, laughing, and well-being.

So that when we see and experience the return of the out-dated negative-1-energy in 202**1**, we can say "*NO*". This is not how we want it to be.

We hated the lockdowns, and we hated the loss of work, but we loved making the funny videos. And we loved caring about others because it made us feel special and that gave meaning to our lives. And living a meaningful life is what being human is all about.

Surely we can say: We want to return to the loving 2020 world, but without the hardship of COVID-19.

Don't let the hardships of this time be in vein.

Having gone through such a major disruption to our lives, this is the perfect time to really make long-term permanent conscious changes to our world when we come out the other side.

Think about how scientists worldwide have been cooperating in the search for a COVID-19 vaccine—cooperating in a way never before experienced. Why couldn't that cooperation continue?

Even politicians are working together as one in deciding what is best for their citizens, rather than just focusing on themselves and their parties. Why couldn't that cooperation continue?

And many people are calling for a totally new global economic system. Perhaps a totally Sustainable Green Economy, something like "An Economy for the Common Good" and /or the Modern Monetary Theory economic model where no one is ever out of work. As I mentioned at the beginning of this chapter I talk about all this in *Conscious Economic Sustainability: Equality and an Ethically Sustainable Financial System in Our Post-COVID World.*

Activity 12: Cpt 19—Our Post-COVID World Opportunities—Your Ideas

Take some time out before moving on.

Just sit quietly and relax and let your mind run free and just imagine the ideal sort of a planet you would like to see in our Post-COVID world.

1. First make a list of how you'd like your personal Post-COVID world to be.

2. Then a list of your work-related Post-COVID world.

3. And a list of our ideal global-planetary Post-COVID world.

4. At some stage come back and turn those lists into a narrative form of writing using full VAKOG (Visual, Auditory, Kinaesthetic, Olfactory, Gustatory) descriptors to bring those visions of yours to life.

5. As a Conscious Leader of Change—list all the actions you can take to make your visions a reality.

6. Perhaps you could share your visions with your like-minded friends in the form of a group visioning party. Now that really is powerful, as the notion of global consciousness demonstrates.

7. Finally, keep adding to your lists and every now and again send your suggestions to me at support@ConsciousChangeToday.com so I can share those ideas with other like-minded people.

I began this chapter by saying: Nearly 40 years ago, in my 'Power of Two' paper, I said that from 2020 on, we'd begin to live in a totally different world.

And we will.

The time is now. The choice is ours. It's up to each and every one of us to choose to live a conscious loving life in harmony with the cosmic **2** energies supported by global consciousness.

Finally, as a matter of interest the most successful countries at dealing with COVID, with the least number of infections and deaths, are countries led by women. These include Taiwan whose President is Tsai Ing-wen; New Zealand's Prime Minister is Jacinda Ardern; Germany, led by Angela Merkel; and Finland led by Prime Minister Sanna Marin. All are offering a totally different style of leadership.

And this feminine-We-energy leadership is not just appropriate at this time of COVID. It'll be essential for our climate change days ahead.

~ Chapter 20 ~
Climate Change

If all the insects were to disappear from the earth,
within 50 years all life on earth would end. If all
human beings disappeared from the earth, within
50 years all other forms of life would flourish.

~ Jonas Salk ~

S o far in this Part Two, we've looked at some of the most important issues affecting our world today—issues that require as many of us as possible to work towards a significant Conscious Change Today! A change in culture from a *Me* culture to a *We* culture.

And the last but by no means least important issue to highlight is climate change because our world urgently needs conscious ***We not Me*** environmental sustainability.

Climate Change is yet another prime example of the misguided, superior #1, *Me* culture that must move to a healing *We* focus.

I was in my early 20s when the land and the environment took on a new "We" meaning for me. This was a spiritual meaning as opposed to what had previously been a more commercial "Me" perspective.

This spiritual perspective was the result of spending a year or so alone, except for my two dogs Freddie, an Old English Sheepdog, and my first Airedale, Samson. We were living on the banks of the Barcoo River in Australia's harsh Outback, in South Western Queensland, on the edge of the Simpson Desert.

At night I slept in my swag (aka bedroll) under a canopy of black velvet studded with diamonds. And by day I'd watch the pelicans swimming up and down the Barcoo as if they'd been trained by the world's leading choreographer. Maybe they had been.

I also caught "wild" donkeys and trucked them to city sanctuaries on the coast, to prevent them from being shot as vermin.

It was during this time in Outback Queensland that I had a major Road to Damascus experience discovering that of all of the creatures out there, I—"a superior human"—was the most inferior creature around.

I learned that humans are definitely *a part of* nature (a **We** focus) and certainly not *apart from* nature (a **Me** focus). This insightful and also spiritual experience, as opposed to what had previously been a more commercial view of our natural environment, awakened my consciousness to the importance of caring for our natural world and it eventually led to my environmental academic journey. I wanted to get an *academic* understanding of nature, to match my *practical* life experience, so that I could talk in a credible manner to people on all levels about the importance of sustainable living.

Yet it was in the mid-1980s, during my talk-radio/pre academic days, that I began talking about the dangers of a changing climate born of our *Me* attitudes.

Today, climate change is another of the many ways our planet is saying enough is enough. And in *Conscious Environmental Sustainability* I cover many of the issues that need our great concern, understanding, and help. These include the urgent need for Environmental Affirmative Action.[32] We must also change from focusing on one of the most negative of emotions, fear—the fear of climate change—and instead learn to love nature and the environment. We're far less likely to damage what we genuinely love.

In *Conscious Environmental Sustainability: Saving Our Planet through the LOVE of Nature, instead of the FEAR of Climate Change* I also go into climate change in a lot more depth than I will in this chapter. And so if you have even the slightest concern about Climate Change, I do hope that you'll not only take a look at *Conscious Environmental Sustainability,* but also *BECOME A Conscious Environmentalist.*

Something to Think About

Suffice to say that at this time on our blue planet Climate Change is real and it is here with us. And if you think COVID is bad, just wait until you're personally affected by some of the severe effects of Climate Change like those poor people that I spoke about in Chapter 9 who went through month after month after month of uncontrollable bush fires on the East

Coast of Australia in 2019/2020. Or homes around the world that are falling into the water under the siege of rising tides and rougher seas.

During a speech about the Cold War that ran from the mid-to-late 1900s, President Ronald Reagan said:

> We're at war with the most dangerous enemy that has ever faced mankind in his long climb from the swamp to the stars. And it's been said if we ever lose that war, and in so doing lose this way of freedom of ours, history will record with the greatest astonishment that those who had the most to lose did the least to prevent its happening.

Never have truer words been said about Climate Change either. Thank you President Reagan.

Taking a broader view of overall environmental destruction, according to the 2016 *Living Planet Report*,[33] we humans are currently "using the resources of 1.6 planets to provide the goods and services we demand each year".

Unfortunately, we only have 1.0 planet and we have no right to use 160% of that single planet's 100% resources, even if that was possible. Indeed, we don't even have the right to use 100% of the Earth's 100% of resources.

Who do we think we are? And more to the point, how stupid are we to destroy the only planet we have? I don't know about you, but living in a space suit on Mars for the rest of my life isn't at all appealing. And with our current attitudes, we'd destroy that too and then what? Move on to Jupiter and fall through the gaseous clouds?

From a purely anthropocentric, or human-centred perspective, if nothing else, without a healthy environment we can't have a healthy life, or a healthy society, or for that matter a healthy economy. And this is where the systemic nature of sustainability comes in.

As with all systems, while the three arms of sustainability—the environmental, the social, and the economic—can be worked on and studied independently, all three are also totally inter-dependent—they all impact on each other as is evident in the previous chapter with COVID.

Decisions to take care of the environment and ease climate change by, as an example, putting an end to all coal mining, will almost certainly have a negative short-term impact on the *economy*, both nationally and for the local community involved. Also in the short-term, this will adversely affect *society*, especially the local community.

However, ending coal mining will definitely *benefit nature*. And in the long-term, that will also *benefit society*, due to a healthier environment, which will *benefit the economy*. It's all inter-dependent. Everything impacts on everything else. It's all about short-term versus long-term thinking.

Short-Term versus Long-Term Thinking

Short-term versus long-term thinking is how I explain why it has taken decades for most people to begin to even show an interest in the environment and by extension climate change.

On a day-to-day basis, people are more concerned with paying their rent or mortgage and putting food on the table—which is totally understandable. As a result, the economy is seen as a far more pressing issue than the environment.

As I mentioned at the start of the previous chapter, while ignoring environmental issues will be catastrophic, it won't happen tomorrow. Whereas you could get COVID tomorrow and die.

What will receive your greatest attention?

It's true that the current life-changing coronavirus issues must be foremost in our minds and dealt with immediately. But that doesn't mean that in the background climate change is not still building, and building, and building, and building.

And for the thirty-three people who died and thousands who lost their homes in the recent Australian bush fires, climate change *was* experienced in a short-term, first hand way. Although for all too many, it was still just a short-term bush fire not long-term climate change at work.

Demonstrating that our Australian government is able to walk and chew gum at the same time; at the end of June, 2020, in the middle of all the chaos and expense of the pandemic, the Australian Prime Minister announced that the government would spend $270 billion on increasing the size of our military. He said: "We have to be prepared and ready to frame the world in which we live as best as we can, and be prepared to respond and play our role to protect Australia."

Now many skeptics say the announcement was merely to divert everyone's focus away from COVID. And that might or might not be true.

But if our Prime Minister genuinely wanted to "… be prepared and ready to respond and play our role to protect Australia" he would be spending $270 billion on Climate Change initiatives.

In a television interview many years ago, the much-loved American singer-songwriter, actor, activist, and humanitarian, John Denver, who was extremely concerned about the environment, once proposed a very thought-provoking idea. He said that all it would take to heal our environment would be first a change in human attitudes. Then the total amount of money spent on defence, globally, for the following three years should instead be spent on restoring the past damage to the environment and setting up sustainable living practices, globally, for the future. And that would probably still work today.

Again, I know it sounds like asking you to believe in unicorns; but believe me as I've said before, unicorns are starting to make a comeback. And this is where you come in.

Climate Change, Conscious Change, and Feminine-Energy

Climate Change is definitely the result of #1, economic attitudes. Attitudes born of a negative #1 masculine culture. A "superior" patriarchal culture supported by the masculine era of the 1000 — millennium and based on a *ME* culture or focus.

However, the really exciting part is that with our current rising #2 feminine-energy, which is all about a *WE* culture, there's never been a time when cosmic consciousness, or cosmic energy, has been more supportive of all of us working together [*feminine-energy of partnerships and co-operation*] to change the world [*feminine-energy of creativity and innovation*] into a more loving, *WE*-focused, world in which *we* [*feminine-2-energy*] take care of the environment [*feminine-energy of loving actions and love consciousness*].

From an ethical perspective alone, conscious sustainability can't be just considered an add-on. It must be at the heart of absolutely *every* decision made, and *every* action taken, on *all* levels of society.

After all, ethical/conscious sustainability is a virtue and like all virtues (Conscious Intelligence Competency ~ Step 5) it must be integrated into your life and demonstrated unconditionally, 24/7. In other words, it should become an automatic consideration, a given, that both long-term and short-term sustainability impacts are consciously incorporated into all decisions and actions.

Now it's true that this can be very difficult without supportive government policies, which is why it might be time for a brand-new political system along with a new economic system.

The survival of our planet's inhabitants—human and non-human—could well depend on it.

What We've Learned from COVID

The first and most obvious thing COVID has taught us is how to live "together" even if we have to be apart. I invite you to go back to the previous chapter and reflect on all the positive #2 feminine-energy ways that as a global society we instinctively adopted. We must keep those positive COVID attitudes going.

The other thing it's taught us is that the economy does not always *have* to come first.

Normally, the diagram of what's commonly known as the "Triple Bottom Line" is drawn as an equilateral triangle with the economy perched proudly on the top and the social and environmental across the base-line as in the following figure.

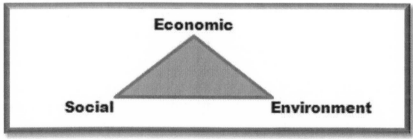

Traditional Triple Bottom Line Diagram

However for over thirty years, I've always presented an inverted triangle with the environment at the point and the social and economic at either end of the "base-line", which is at the top. This is to remind my audiences and my students that keeping our environment healthy is a very fine balancing act. And without a healthy environment, the social and the economic will always come crashing down as COVID has shown us.

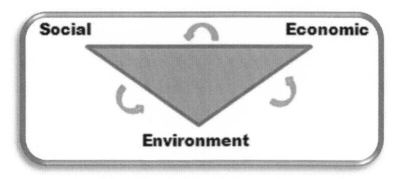

Dr. Kashonia's Conscious Sustainability Version

The arrows in the diagram indicate systems-thinking, reminding us that everything is constantly impacting on everything else.

You'll recall me saying how humans might be able to kill everything from a mouse to an elephant. But a virus, unseen with the naked eye, could kill us all. Perhaps we're not as smart as we thing we are.

And in the past when I was teaching this Ethical/Conscious Sustainability model I never had a real-life example that would really bring the model to life. But today I have a better example than I could have ever imagined — COVID-19.

Yes it's true that up until the coronavirus hit the world, the economic was always thought to be supreme — like most humans erroneously think they are supreme. But then, globally, the leaders of most countries realised that no matter what the economic cost, society had to come first or too many people would die.

And what happened in those countries where the national leader decided that the economy was still number **1** and so restrictions were eased, or not even imposed? More and more people did die. Even so, some leaders didn't mind the people they were representing dying because of their policies. They thought a higher number of deaths was better than negatively hurting their economy—no doubt so long as those deaths didn't include their own death.

Yet there's always an alternative! Develop a new form of economic system with a focus on a conscious sustainability way of life.

So surely this is the ideal time to reflect on our current, out-dated global economic system and as I said in the previous chapter, design an economy where we can have healthy humans, a healthy economy, and a healthy environment. It is possible with a *we not me* mindset. This is something I talk about in both *Conscious Economic Sustainability: Equality and an Ethically Sustainable Financial System in Our Post-COVID World* and also *Conscious Environmental Sustainability: Saving Our Planet through the LOVE of Nature, instead of the FEAR of Climate Change.*

And COVID has taught us that if the emergency is great enough, for most countries the social will come before the economy. Even so, the environment is still left lagging behind yet it's our fundamental abuse of nature that is arguably at the heart of the problem.

The more we destroy the natural habitat of wildlife, the more the wildlife will encroach on human domains because there's nowhere else for them to go. And so the more likely we humans are to become infected with viruses that the wildlife can tolerate but humans can't.

COVID-19 isn't the last pandemic any of us will see or hear about. And all the pandemics we've seen in recent years have cost a fortune in economic terms. But we're still not prepared to look at our human abuse of nature because deadly neo-classical capitalism is still in control.

And it's climate change that's a far greater threat than COVID to our global society, and our current form of global economy. Again due to the human abuse of nature being driven by capitalism being in control.

If politicians thought the environment was the number one public concern, as they currently do with COVID-19, they'd be onto it in a flash.

So why isn't climate change our number one public concern!

Believe me, COVID will seem like kindergarten stuff, socially and economically, when the full force of Climate Change is affecting us all on a daily basis. And before too long maybe the climate will be in such a pickle that the climate will become our number one concern.

Maybe COVID-19 was just a practice run for us all.

Maybe COVID was saying enough is enough. But are we going to listen?

So just imagine for a moment what our physical, environmental world would be like if the same passion, energy, focus, money, and overall resources that are currently being spent combating COVID-19, were spent on the environment, climate change, and our overall abuse of nature in all its forms.

With COVID all we could do was wash our hands, wear a mask, and physically-distance, often in a depressing lockdown situation.

By contrast, if the same attention and money was given to the environment and climate change as has been given to COVID the opportunity for community participation in environmentally enhancing activities is limited only by our very fertile and creative imaginations. Instead of having to cope with a depressing lockdown situation, we could all work together in the most positive, creative, and life enhancing ways imaginable giving all our lives great meaning.

~ Chapter 21 ~
2020 and Beyond

*Not enough people in this world carry a cosmic
perspective with them. Yet it could be life-changing.*
~ Neil deGrasse Tyson ~

A s you know, my original "Power of Two" paper and
this book have looked at each decade through to 2020.
Well it's now 2020, so how do I see the future
decades playing out from here?

First, as I've said before nothing changes overnight short
of an environmental catastrophe (or a pandemic and that *is*
arguably environmental). These changes have a beginning in
the previous year, or decade, and then take some years to
become integrated into the socio-cultural way things are done.
So with that qualification in mind, let's take a glimpse at what
might possibly lie ahead.

The 2020s and beyond have the potential to support more
and more women in their quest to do more and more amazing
things. With an equally special role for "transformed" men.

However, look what happens in 202**1**, the old negative
masculine energy 1 reappears. And if the negative masculine-
energy bullies were doing all they could to cling to power in

the last decade (2010-2019), this will be their very last hurrah for another ten years. So all hell could break loose in 2021.

And I can't help but continually reflect on the fact that it will most likely be 2021 that the mopping-up after COVID will have to take place. And as I mentioned in passing in the COVID chapter, for most places that mopping-up will be done using very masculine energy if it's done in 2021.

But after that, the 2 energy in 2022 will be able to repair a lot of the 2021 damage from two perspectives.

First, because 2 is the number of the peacemaker, it's the energy best able to resolve conflicts and difficult situations. Therefore it will be well supported, metaphysically, to resolve the conflicts from 2021.

Then from a different perspective, the universal number of the year 2022 is 6; or 2+2+2=6. And you might recall from my review of the 1960s, 6 is the number for the humanitarian. It's also the number of love, and peace, and family, and learning, and friendship.

From there, to get a feel for the continuing decades after 2022, just see what the main decade-number-themes were for the decades 1920 to 1990 in Appendix A. The same decade-number-themes will apply in the 2020s, 2030s, 2040s and so on. Although those new decades will all have the beautiful millennium 2 feminine-energy foundation, instead of being underpinned by the negative masculine/patriarchal millennium 1.

Meanwhile, again it's important to remember that while the universe is doing its part by providing this loving cosmic energy on a metaphysical level, it can't fully make these very special transformations here on the Earth on its own. To bring that love and peace and harmony to fruition in our physical world, it needs us all to work together — and that includes you.

And we don't have a lot of time now

Who knows, by the time you read this book 2022 might already have arrived.

But if we all work together and make 2022 the exceptionally beautiful year that the cosmic 2 energy will support, and if the past trends continue, then the years that follow should look something like this.

As global consciousness continues to focus on the 2000s, the millennium 2 energy will continue to strengthen for the next thousand years, as did the masculine 1 over the last thousand years.

The decade 2 with all its loving and peaceful attributes will also strengthen over the next ten years, getting us off to a great start, especially in 2022, with its three 2s. And for the years 2023 − 2029, again look in Appendix A to get an idea of what the numbers 3 − 9 represent.

And within that 2 decade, after a year of conflict resolution in 2022, with "3" being the number of imagination, creativity, and artistic pursuits, 2023 will begin to implement creative endeavours that enhance the growth of beauty, peace, and happiness on the planet.

My only concern here is that the growing effects of climate change could well take its toll in an equally "creative",

albeit negative, manner. And that could definitely be the case by the time the 2030s arrive.

Although on the other hand, it might be those negative effects of climate change that help to bring us all together by 2023/2030.

We might all work as one for a new world, with new loving attitudes, actions, and mind-sets. That sort of thing has happened before.

Allow me to share this one example of a positive side to a negative situation, because it's a favourite of mine.

For decades, at a political inter-government level, the United Nations Environment Program (UNEP) has worked on their Mediterranean Action Plan initiative, aimed at cleaning the pollution in the Mediterranean Sea.

And yes, UNEP's work is commendable. But despite, or perhaps because of their reports, and conventions, and meetings, and protocols, and so on, they haven't done a great job with the Mediterranean.

By contrast, each year hundreds of thousands of concerned citizens from twenty-two countries, covering three different continents, *peacefully* join forces and are successfully cleaning up the pollution in the Mediterranean Sea. Yet politically, many of the countries that these people come from are fighting each other to the death — literally.

But on the level of the individual citizen, in the main they're all the same no matter what's happening politically in their home country. They all want lives of peace, equality, happiness, and a clean and healthy environment.

So once again, the people have the power to take things into their own hands and make a real difference despite the politics and the wars they're having to live with, propagated by their weak, insecure, frequently corrupt, male leaders.

I often used to say the fastest way to world peace would be if we were invaded by little green Martians, because instead of fighting each other, we'd all come together to fight the Martians. Perhaps the coronavirus is our global little green Martian invaders bringing us all together, working as one.

But instead of coming together to fight the Martians, or COVID, how much better would it be if we all came together by harnessing the beautiful power and characteristics of the

2-millennium energies. How much better it would be if we all helped do some major climate change mitigation and environmental restoration; or focused on world peace, or global equality, or the like.

If your spirit is willing, harnessing those 2 energies is so easy to do.

Living in Harmony with # 2

This time I'd like to start this section by calling upon what's known as Pascal's Wager, put forth by the 17th century scientist, mathematician, and philosopher Blaise Pascal.

Pascal's Wager goes like this:

Pascal was asked if God exists. To which he replied that he didn't know and no one could say for sure. But in case God did exist, Pascal recommended that people always act in an ethical way to ensure they go to heaven. And even if God didn't exist, by acting ethically they've lived a good and happy life. So either way a win.

So if you ask me: Kashonia, are you sure that the global consciousness-born energy of the number 2 in this new 2000-millennium will continue to play out as you've suggested? My answer has to be no, I'm not *sure*.

While I can be sure the patterns and resulting trends have been accurate for the past 100+ years; who really knows what's ahead — even tomorrow. And COVID has certainly taught us that.

At the start of 2020 did you ever even imagine that within a few weeks the entire planet would be in a global legal lockdown situation???

But if the years ahead do continue to follow the past decade-number-correlations, then the following guidelines are going to be well worth considering.

As Pascal said with reference to God, if the years ahead do not follow past patterns, then at least following his ethical guidelines will ensure that you live a happy, peaceful, and successful life, both individually and as part of your local and global community.

But first, Pascal's Wager always reminds me of a belief in some circles today.

Keep in mind that science tells us that everything on Earth, including us humans, are influenced by various forms of harmonic electrical energy, like the Schumann Resonances. Based on that, there are those people who suggest that when someone refuses to live in harmony with the prevailing cosmic energies (in this current case the 2 energies) they'll be living in dis-harmony with the new global/cosmic energies.

And unless people make some significant changes in their lives, living a life of dis-harmony will lead to accelerated dis-ease resulting in a significant increase in deaths due to things like cancer, cardio-vascular problems, diabetes, and the like.

Is that scenario true? I have no idea, but I'm sure Pascal would love it.

And a final word of warning. We all need to be constantly alert to any new bursts of negative masculine energy trying to emerge and regain power, especially in 20**21**. So see how you can join with others to stop it by promoting more acceptable conscious alternatives.

~ Chapter 22 ~
Your Call to Action ~
The Time is NOW

The future depends on what you do today.
~ Mahatma Gandhi ~

As I've demonstrated time and time again throughout this book, there's an undeniable link between COVID, Climate Change, and the Rise of Feminine-Energy. COVID and Climate Change are saying enough is enough of the negative masculine-1-energy and the associated *Me* attitudes found in our current economic system. An outdated, unsustainable, and so unethical system of growth economic capitalism that believes it is totally superior to the natural world on which all of our very lives depend.

At the beginning of every semester of my MBA leadership classes I'd put a challenge out to my students. The challenge was that they had a whole semester to think of just one thing that didn't ultimately depend on a healthy environment. Over the years, talking to thousands of students, not one student was able to successfully answer the challenge.

Not only is that negative economic system outdated because it was a temporary system that's lingered on for nearly 100 years. But a system that definitely became outdated when we entered our new **2**000-*We*-focused millennium.

And this is where the link between COVID, climate change, and the rise of feminine-energy comes in. Because it's the positive-**2**-*We*-focused-energy that we've been given at this time that can come to nature's urgent rescue. And rescuing nature is the only way we can rescue ourselves.

So Your Call to Action is this:

Women need to embrace the basics of Conscious Feminism—see Chapter 16. Even if you hate the word feminism just focus on the conscious part.

Men need to find the courage to embrace their feminine-2-energy if they are to succeed in this 21st century—be that at home, at work, or within the world at large.

And remember, I'm talking about feminine-*energy* not femininity. So those loving actions are just basic Conscious Intelligence, ethics-in-action, competencies.

After all, most heterosexual women want their heterosexual men to be men. But men in a nice, loving, conscious—**We *not Me*** way.

So men, you need to live a life of Conscious Masculinity—see Chapter 17. And when you do, this can be the most exciting time of your life, if you let it.

And do keep in mind that these transformations will initially be harder for many men than for women. And they'll be a total breeze for Gen Zs.

Together we all need to live a life in which we harness the energetic power of our new 2000-millennium. And living in harmony with that cosmic force will no doubt lead to a more peaceful, loving, and most importantly, sustainable world — *a more conscious world*.

As it was with COVID — we're all in this together. Buckminster Fuller spoke about living on Spaceship Earth. We all need to take action. Nothing will change if you're not prepared to help.

As I explained at the end of the last chapter, that harmonic energy is calling on as many people around the world as possible to start "living in harmony with our 2 energies" that were born of the continual global focus on the 2000s of global consciousness.

In other words, it's a call to raise your levels of conscious intelligence competencies with a focus on cultivating a conscious-*We* way of living and working. It's a call to habituate as many appropriate loving, moral, *We*, virtues as possible. It's a call to take-heed of the various suggestions made throughout this book.

And do keep in mind the positive working together *We* attitudes we saw during the 1st Wave of COVID-19 — see Chapter 19.

Because as the Lorax said:

UNLESS someone like *YOU* cares a whole awful lot,

Nothing gets better. No it will not.

Now the Lorax was not being specific. That's what's so wonderful about our world. We're all different and so our make-a-difference passions will also be different. The key is to ensure that they have a foundation of conscious, *me to we*, living.

Maybe you might just choose to live a conscious everyday personal life and choose to develop *conscious* feminism traits.

Or you might choose to develop conscious masculinity attitudes and mindsets.

Perhaps you might just choose to live a conscious everyday life at work and within your community.

Or you might choose to work with others and help them live conscious, *me to we*, lives.

Or you might choose to become a conscious leader of change in whatever area makes your heart sing the loudest and focus on helping develop the loving, peaceful, and sustainable world that so many people would love to see *and our natural world is now demanding*.

And if you've made it this far, I'll assume that you like me, are one of those people who would like to see some form of conscious change either throughout *your* world or even *the* world. In which case, whether you realise it or not, you are now at a choice point. Do you take action or do you basically dismiss all you've read.

Indeed …

We are all at a choice point

Have you heard about the concept of "Choice Point"? In case you haven't, let me explain. And if you are familiar with the concept, it's always worth a review from what might be a different perspective.

Choice Point

In 2012, a movie length documentary, *Choice Point*[34], came out. The doco describes what can be very special times in our personal lives and also special times on the planet when the situation, or the time, or the energy, call it what you will, is such that it's very supportive of making major transformational changes. These are the points in time when we have to make a choice.

We can choose to do nothing and keep going with the same-old, same-old. Or we can choose to make a major difference in our life, especially if the time is right and there's an external supporting force — as there arguably is at this time.

People like Sir Richard Branson, Archbishop Desmond Tutu, John Paul DeJoria, Jack Canfield, Gregg Braden, and Barbara Marx Hubbard, were all interviewed in the movie, and all agreed:

> Their transformation was not only personal but also collective, because as they reached their goals and bettered their own lives, they also shared their gifts with the world, and continue to do so, making major positive social contributions[35].

The notion of choice point came from the work of quantum physicist, Hugh Everett III, the man who proposed the many worlds theory so widely accepted by quantum physicists these days.

If you've seen the doco-drama *What the Bleep*, you'd be familiar with the theory that parallel worlds might exist in different dimensions all at the same time. I know that sounds wild, but so does having parallel lines cross. And as I always say if you can't categorically disprove an idea, then it's sheer arrogance to dismiss it out of hand. Now that doesn't mean it's right. But it also doesn't mean that it's wrong either.

So the question is; which "parallel world" are you going to choose to live on?

And you do have a number of choices.

(1) You can sit back and say everything that has happened that mirrors the characteristics of each decade-number as described is purely coincidental — *I'm not interested.*

Now as Pascal would say, that's not a good idea for a bright personal future. And once again I have to ask, how many times does a "coincidence" have to occur before that "coincidence" is given some legitimate credence?

OR

(2) You can sit back and say well things have been evolving on their own in a sort of fashion; let it all continue that way — *I'm not interested.*

And then you can continue to do whatever you've been doing. But again, this is where you might have problems, as I indicated earlier.

OR

(3) You can take to the streets with your new-found 2 energy and enthusiasm and think you're making a big difference. And maybe you are, or maybe you're not, or maybe you're making a difference in an inappropriate manner, like the  shocking idea of calling on women to go out and "kill rapists".

OR

(4) You can give some deep thought (Conscious Intelligence Competencies ~ Step 7) to what is actually happening in the world, as well as in your personal life, and take ***appropriate*** action and ***really*** make a difference to your life, your world, and maybe even our entire world starting by living in harmony with our 2 energies. In other words, living a conscious life.

But at least you're now aware that you can *choose* to demonstrate any of the many moral virtues/loving actions/positive feminine-energy characteristics/ conscious change characteristics, in any way, at any time. And when you do; know that the cosmic energetic vibrations that affect us all will be supporting you on a meta-physical level, regardless of whether or not you believe in those cosmic energies.

No matter which choice you make, following are some steps to guide you on your journey.

Stage 1 – Your Relationship with Yourself

Perhaps you'll choose to just dip your toe in the water at this time and begin with what I sometimes call The Oxygen Mask level. This is a bit like putting your own oxygen mask on in the aeroplane before you begin to help others around you. And in the Conscious Intelligence Competency Framework this is your relationship with yourself—Steps 1, 2, and 3—because often before you can make a difference to *the* world, you have to make a difference to *your own* world first.

This can certainly be done at the same time as you're working on a make-a-difference project at a higher level for your community, or the world at large. But enriching your relationship with yourself is certainly an important area to *continually* work on.

In *Conscious Intelligence Competencies* (Book 2), I'll introduce you to these foundation conscious intelligence competencies (Steps 1 to 3). However the *Conscious Intelligence Competencies* companion volume, Book 3 in the Conscious Change Series of Books—*Conscious Self-Discovery: Enriching Your Relationship with Yourself,* greatly expands on those first three foundation competencies.

And in 2021, I'm thinking of setting up a special interactive online program based around the *Conscious Self-Discovery* book. So I invite you to subscribe to my mailing list so you can find out when it's released. Just go to

https://www.consciouschangetoday.com/subscribe/

The time is now
The choice is yours
It's up to you

As Michael Jackson sang in 1987

> I'm starting with me
>
> I'm starting with the man in the mirror
>
> I'm asking him to change his ways
>
> And no message could have been any clearer
>
> If you wanna make the world a better place
>
> Take a look at yourself and then make a change

And if you'd really like to make a difference at a higher level ~ "you wanna make the world a better place" and become a Conscious Leader of Change. Then continue with the next stage — Preparation.

Stage 2 ~ A Conscious Leader of Change—Preparation

Let's say you've chosen to go on a two-week vacation. Well you don't wait until day one arrives and then just walk out your front door with no idea of where you're going, or what you'll be doing.

Obviously you have to do some preparation. You might have to book some accommodation. Will you be driving there or have to take a plane? What sort of clothes will you have to pack? And so on.

Well if you want to make a difference, be that within your home, or workplace, or community, or beyond, you must do some preparation. And that's one reason why I wrote the second book in this Conscious Change Series of Books, *Conscious Intelligence Competencies: Taking Emotional Intelligence to the Next Level for Our 21st Century World of Relationships ~ with Yourself and Others, in Business, with the Planet, and Beyond.*

So let's take a look at four essential keys in this preparatory stage.

Key #1 ~ Raise your Conscious Intelligence Competencies

In Chapter 1, I spoke about a student in one of my Hong Kong MBA Leadership classes, Chen, who after learning many of these Conscious Intelligence Competencies, went home and was able to completely change the home life he and his family were sharing. Whatever sort of make-a-difference endeavour you think you might pursue; these competencies are the basic building blocks.

Say you want to build a beautiful new two storey house. You don't just start with the pretty walls and a roof. It must have a solid foundation or you'll come to grief very rapidly. The same applies to changing the world—making a difference—in a conscious or ethical manner. You must start with a solid foundation. And at least some understanding of the Conscious Intelligence Competencies is essential or like the house with no solid foundation, you could come to grief very rapidly.

Key #2 ~ Imagination

Key number 2 is where you start day-dreaming, and maybe some night dreaming too, about that forthcoming vacation. Or in this case, imagining where you'd like to begin using your Conscious Leader of Change skills.

So let's begin with a few words from Albert Einstein and then a little later is an activity about imagining your future conscious world.

Albert Einstein said: "Imagination is more important than knowledge. For knowledge is limited to all we now know and understand, while imagination embraces the entire world, and all there ever will be to know and understand".

The only thing I always add to Einstein's comment is that the knowledge and understanding is also very important as a foundation, so that your imagination is able to take off from a much higher platform and so soar to even greater heights. It's all about standing on the shoulders of giants and going from there.

To help your imagining, just keep working on Stage 1 above, and as you do, you might be surprised with the ideas that come to mind.

Meanwhile, apart from addressing personal issues and needs, from a global perspective the average rational person when asked, wants to see a more peaceful, loving, ethical, and these days, sustainable world—a more conscious world.

And that's exactly the kind of world we'd have if all nearly 8 billion of us acted in a more peaceful, loving, ethical, and sustainable manner. Surely you can't argue with that logic. The problem comes with how to have that happen.

The good news is that we don't need all 8 billion of us to act that way to affect a tipping point. According to Everett Rogers, the author of the highly acclaimed book, *Diffusion of Innovation,* if change is capable of happening then all it takes is around 15% of us to take action to get that little old snowball in motion.

Now this might sound as if I'm asking you, once again, to believe in unicorns. But with only about 15% of people 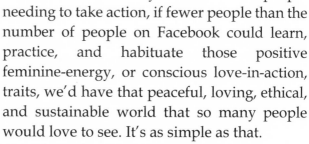 needing to take action, if fewer people than the number of people on Facebook could learn, practice, and habituate those positive feminine-energy, or conscious love-in-action, traits, we'd have that peaceful, loving, ethical, and sustainable world that so many people would love to see. It's as simple as that.

The amazing opportunities for men, women, and non-binary at this time are enormous. Because even if we just adopt and habituate those conscious *me to we* traits with the aim of helping our planet and all who live here (*me to we),* our own personal lives will automatically be beautifully transformed in the process as well.

To help you imagine what a conscious, loving, and peaceful world might be like, see if the words to John Lennon's greatest solo hit provide some inspiration for the next activity. I'm sure you know the tune. So sing the words, even if just to yourself, in your mind. It will have an even greater effect.

Imagine there's no heaven
It's easy if you try
No hell below us
Above us only sky
Imagine all the people
Living for today...

Imagine there's no countries
It isn't hard to do
Nothing to kill or die for
And no religion too
Imagine all the people
Living life in peace...

You may say I'm a dreamer
But I'm not the only one
I hope someday you'll join us
And the world will be as one

Imagine no possessions
I wonder if you can
No need for greed or hunger
A brotherhood of man
Imagine all the people
Sharing all the world...

You may say I'm a dreamer
But I'm not the only one
I hope someday you'll join us
And the world will live as one

Activity 13: Cpt 22—Imagine a Conscious, Loving, & Peaceful World

This activity might be about your world at home, at work, or the broader world itself. So just adapt the following guidelines to suit whatever project you have in mind.

Begin by taking a few minutes to imagine what *the* world (or *your* world) would be like if everyone acted in a loving, conscious ~ *we not me* way.

The next three questions might help to direct your focus. Make sure you write your answers down.

1. What is it in your world, or even *the* world that you passionately believe needs changing?

2. What skills and talents do you have that you enjoy using the most?

3. How could you use those special skills and talents to make a difference to the project you noted in question #1?

Make sure that you use your creative imagination when answering those questions. And creativity and creative imagination is the companion competency to critical thinking—Competency 7 of the Conscious Intelligence Competency Framework.

Also, at some time write up your imagined world in narrative/story form using full VAKOG (Visual, Auditory, Kinaesthetic, Olfactory, Gustatory) descriptors to bring that world to life.

Share your vision with others.

Perhaps you could get your friends together and have a group imagining session. Now that really is powerful as the notion of global/field-consciousness demonstrates.

Key #3 ~ Give Your Life Meaning or Purpose

On a number of occasions now I've spoken about the benefits of living a meaningful life. And the key to living a meaningful life is to make a contribution, or make a difference, to something or someone beyond or greater than ourselves.

Indeed, making a contribution to others is one of the key needs that all humans have. And every time we come from the heart and put ethics-into-action (Conscious Intelligence Competency 5) by demonstrating one of those conscious virtues, that's exactly what we're doing. We're making a difference to someone or something outside of our self — *We not Me*.

There's an abundance of research showing us that when we live a meaningful life the personal benefits that result are enormous.

And remember that you can still live a *we not me* life, and yet still receive personal benefits. It's all about ensuring that your focus and intention are on *we not me*. In other words, you're doing the activity from a totally unconditional perspective.

So here are just some of the benefits to living a meaningful life.

Not only will living a meaningful life make you feel good and increase your happiness and well-being, but that in turn leads to added longevity; greatly improved physical health and so well-being; a stronger immune system; greatly improved psychological health and so well-being; more positive emotions; better personal, business, and community relationships; a greater ability to become financially secure and more productive and creative at work; improved leadership and negotiation skills; you're more likely to get married or have a stable personal partnership; have more social support; more friends; be more philanthropic and kinder to others; have greater resilience; live a more loving life; live a more ethical life; and enjoy greater overall success in life whatever success means to you.

WOW! WOW! WOW!

Surely that's something to think about and aim for.

And living a meaningful life is all about living a conscious life!

"But", you might say as many people have said to me, "the world is as it is, what can I do to help the world become a more peaceful and loving place when it's controlled by the 1% — the "elite" — those in power?

To which I refer to Gandhi who, speaking from experience, put it this way: "A small body of determined spirits fired by an unquenchable faith in their mission can alter the course of history".

Much later anthropologist, Margret Mead, repeated the same sentiment with these very famous words: "Never doubt that a small group of thoughtful, committed citizens can change the world; indeed, it's the only thing that ever has".

And as you'll recall from the 18th century moral philosopher and virtue ethicist, David Hume: "The general public always have the numbers and so the power to overturn any unjust act if they're willing to exercise that power".

So to help you find that group of like-minded committed citizens with whom you can work to make a difference, let me introduce you to the New Superpower.

The New Superpower

And what's the New Superpower you might well ask?

No, it has nothing to do with the European Union, and it's not China or India. It's yet another concept arguably given to us by this incredible new number 2 millennium — conscious change ~ positive feminine-energy in action.

The label "The New Superpower" was first used in a *New York Times* article in February 2003.[36] Later it became a term that was regularly included in speeches given by the former secretary-general of the United Nations, Kofi Anan.[37]

However in the late 1990s, internationally renowned environmental activist, Paul Hawken, came to the realisation that the world was filled with groups of people who were "as mad as hell" about the direction in which the world was heading. After years of research he discovered the existence of all these citizen-based groups. Once again, the epitome of unity in diversity and 2 energies in action.

And in 2007, Hawken published a book called *Blessed Unrest: How the Largest Movement in the World Came into Being and Why No One Saw it Coming*. He was talking about The New Superpower.

This ever-growing movement of around two million citizen-based groups and NGOs (non-governmental organisations) are active all over the world. Some of these groups have memberships in the dozens; others have memberships in the millions.

The New Superpower is able to occur at this time because of the power of the Internet.

These different groups support a vast array of different interests including children and education, the environment, community development, indigenous peoples and their rights, women's issues, animal rights, human rights, spirituality, and more specific issues such as climate change through to groups focusing on anti-racism, anti-poverty, homelessness, volunteerism, peace, equality, and thousands of other world-changing issues. You name it and there's a group supporting it.

Now if you asked the millions and millions of these New Superpower supporters what sort of underpinning global changes they'd like to see in the world, the vast majority would give a very simple answer. They'd say, in some form or other, that they'd like to see a more ethical, equal, loving, and sustainable world. In other words a more "conscious" world. And that's what they're working to achieve within their specific area of interest. They're working for **Conscious Change Today**.

And if you're reading this book, you're probably already on the mailing list of one or more of these groups. I know I am. So whatever you're passionate about; there'll be a New Superpower-type organisation that will make your heart sing while fanning the flames of your fieriest passions.

To find a directory containing most of these different groups, just go to https://www.guidestar.org/ And if the first group you join isn't ready to stand-up for a major Conscious Change Today, continue searching for a group that is.

And if you're already in a New Superpower group, don't just say "yes" to receiving newsletters, become an *active* member. Encourage your group to work with other groups on developing a strategy that will apply some real heat to the global percolator in their field.

Although virtually nothing has been said in recent years about "The New Superpower" by name, these New Superpower organisations have been quietly continuing to grow, both in number and size.

Remember that none of us can do any of this on our own—alone we're weak, but together we are strong. So become an *active* member of at least one New Superpower organisation.

As John Lennon sang:

> *I hope someday you'll join us*
> *And the world will live as one*

Key #4 ~ Appropriate Action

On a number of occasions I've mentioned that our actions need to be "appropriate" actions. But what is an "appropriate action" in this 21st century conscious world?

Obviously they're **We not Me** focused. And so all appropriate conscious actions have an ethical foundation, with a conscious awareness of the impacts, both positive and negative, that those actions will have on all stakeholders (see Conscious Intelligence Competency 6—Stakeholder Analysis).

And sometimes, even a loving action might be inappropriate, depending on the situation and/or the other party involved.

In Chapter 2, I mentioned a very famous quote from Aristotle that's an excellent guide to whether or not an action is appropriate. It goes like this …

The mark of whether or not an action is *appropriate* is to ensure it's performed at the right time, on the right grounds, towards the right people/person, for the right motive, and in the right way"[38].

An understanding of your Conscious Intelligence Competencies will also guide you here.

Meanwhile, here are some questions that might guide your conscious planning and imagining process in an appropriate manner.

As with most things, you start with the end in mind and go from there. So:

❖ What sort of make-a-difference outcome are you hoping to achieve?

❖ What resources—physical, financial, personal, emotional, social, business, *et cetera*—do you have available to support that outcome?

❖ What are the challenges you might find along the way?

❖ How will you overcome those challenges?

❖ What actions must be taken to achieve your outcome?

❖ How will those actions affect others?

Now start to make some action-oriented decisions with a game plan to suit. In other words it's time to Take Appropriate Action.

Stage 3 ~ Conscious Change Checklist

The world will never be the same on the other side of COVID-19 and the recession. So let's rebuild the new world, in harmony with conscious loving 2 cosmic energies that global consciousness is focusing on—in most cases non-consciously. It's that positive conscious energy that'll support your actions.

The Time is Now

You'll recall me talking about Brexit. And after the Brexit victory so many people were shocked and upset. But they were the same people who didn't bother to vote. If you didn't vote — don't complain.

In 2016, so many Americans were shocked and upset at Donald Trump's victory. But Trump became President on only about 25% of votes from the eligible voting population. What happened to everyone else? If you didn't bother to vote—why not? And if you didn't vote—you can't complain.

UNLESS someone like YOU cares a whole awful lot,
Nothing gets better. No it will not.

Stepping up and actually taking action is what makes a genuine conscious leader of change.

So use this checklist of the main conscious actions that you've read about in the pages of this book and begin implementing *Conscious Change Today*.

✓ CHOICE POINT ~ Are you going to choose to implement conscious change today, or not?

✓ Start living in harmony with our new 2 energies.

✓ Enrich your relationship with yourself – Steps 1 – 3 of the Conscious Intelligence Competencies Framework.

✓ Work on raising all your levels of Conscious Intelligence.

✓ What sort of a world are you imagining — at home, at work, in the community, across the planet, and beyond?

✓ What sort of special, specific, make-a-difference project would you like to work on?

✓ Double check every decision you make and action you take and ensure that they are all "appropriate" actions and decisions.

✓ Find two New Superpower organisations that you can join, today, that will support the project you want to work on.

✓ Give your life meaning by actively supporting those groups.

✓ Make sure you've completed all the activities in this book. You'll find a list of them at the end of the Table of Contents. All the activities are designed to give you some food for thought and a deeper level of understanding of the topic that they appear with.

✓ The most important activity to start working on immediately is Activity 5: in Chapter 16 — What Loving Actions Would You Choose?

Briefly it goes like this:

Don't just look at the list (below) of moral virtues/loving actions/ conscious positive feminine-energy characteristics — call them what you like; but actually *study* the list.

Think about each one and write down the six loving actions that are most appropriate to the sort of life you lead and/or the sort of make-a-difference project you want to work on.

LOVING/CONSCIOUS ACTIONS ~ ETHICAL VIRTUES

These moral virtues/conscious actions include,
but are not limited to:

Empathy, Equality, Respect, Trust, Compassion, Truthfulness, Fairness, Gratitude, Altruism, Kindness, Co-operation, Justice, Giving, Mercy, Peace, Joy, Acceptance, Non-judgement, Sharing, Patience, Courtesy, Generosity, Benevolence, Courage, Temperance, Nurturing, Honesty, Humility, Self-love, Self-control, Ethical/Conscious Sustainability, and Me to We—Conscious Living

---

Begin today to habituate each of the actions on your list by practicing them at every opportunity. And each time you realise that you might have slipped into a negative action or mind-set, something that happens to us all at some time, stop and consciously change that to a positive action or mind-set. This is explained in more detail in the chapter on Selfless Self-Love in *Conscious Self-Discovery*.

Basically, the more of those loving actions you habituate; the more you'll be living a conscious life in harmony with Conscious Femininity, Conscious Masculinity, and the 2 energy; and so the more meaning you'll be adding to your life; and the more wonderful your personal life, and our world, will become.

From little things, big things grow

So what are *you* going to do to help spread love-in-action and see conscious change today around *your* world, and maybe even around *our* world?

Activity 14: Cpt 22—Your New Stories, New World—Appreciative Inquiry[39] Exercise

This is similar to the last activity, however it's more focused and specific and is coming from a slightly different perspective. So when you finish this activity compare your answers to the answers you wrote down in the previous activity.

Start writing about the actions you plan to take. The following steps, based on Appreciative Inquiry, will guide you.

1. Start with a list of the areas you're most passionate about.

2. List all the good things about the way those areas operate in the world today. In other words—*valuing the best of what currently is*.

3. List the things you think could be improved—*envisioning what might be*. Remember to think of the second-order changes too, not only tweaks

4. Talk to other like-minded people about *how it should be*. Again, remember second-order changes—think big.

5. And with your group, or if you're doing this on your own, become very creative about what this new world will be like. How are you all going to make it happen?

6. Set up a step-by-step game plan of what you'll do to put your ideas into action. Make sure your game plan has a time frame for all actions too.

The time is now
The choice is yours
It's up to you

UNLESS someone like <u>you</u>

cares a whole awful lot,

Nothing gets better. No it will not.

And remember...

to register for your free *Conscious Leader's Guide to ~ Living a Meaningful Life ~ Making a Difference;* and the latest news on forthcoming Conscious Change books and Conscious Change workshops. Just go to my Conscious Change Today website.

https://www.ConsciousChangeToday.com/subscribe/

Just a Reminder with Thanks

Thank you so much for reading the book.

I hope you enjoyed it and would like to help me spread this very important message far and wide.

If so, please tell your friends and mailing list about the book and post a note on your blogs and all your social media feeds.

And if you'd like to put a brief review up on the book's Amazon page that would really be wonderful.

Just go to https://tinyurl.com/ConsciousChangeToday

The choice is yours.
It's entirely up to you.

Appendix A: Decade-Number Correlations

A s you're aware, I first explored the following correlations in the 1980s as part of the underpinning research for a paper I called "The Power of Two".

In that paper I speculated that we'd see major changes in the world once we were in the new 2000 millennium, due to the power of global consciousness focusing on the 2000s. And it's the number two that for millennia has been said to promote a right-brain, feminine-energy with the key words being peacemaker, partnerships, co-operation, tact, agreement, diplomacy, love consciousness, consideration, and a spiritual influence, and so on.

I suggested that with the arrival of the 2000s we'd be leaving behind one thousand years strongly influence by the number one, which is a left-brain, masculine number promoting masculine *energy*. Not necessarily men, but *masculine energy*. It's the number of independence, control, domination, aggression, individuality, and egocentrism.

To support my forecast, I initially examined the correlations between the energetic characteristics of the decade-numbers from the 1920s to the 1970s with speculation from the 1980s to the 2020s.

Following is a summary of the decades 1920s to 1990s. Then a large part of this book details the period from 2000 to 2020.

Just as all the decade-numbers, 1920 to 1990, correspond to their decade-number-characteristics, all are still underpinned with the masculine-energy from the 1000 millennium.

However the next 1000 years will be underpinned with the feminine two energy of partnerships, co-operation, and the peacemaker *et cetera*.

It's important to remember that there'll always be a bit of an overlap as one decade ends and the next one starts.

And finally, this is not about hard empirical scientific evidence. It's all about recurring patterns and trends, as is the case with most socio-cultural evidence.

1920s

The number two is considered to be symbolic of the peacemaker, harmony, partnerships, and bringing people together. And the general underpinning trend of the 1920s was a peaceful coming together after the end of World War I which officially ended on November 11th, 1918.

1930s

The number three is about the good things in life, the chameleon, imagination, inspiration, adaptability, emotion, entertainment, and it's especially big on creativity.

However with that in mind, the 1930s are mainly known for the Great Depression which began towards the end of 1929 and continued globally for most of the decade. And while an "elite" few did very well out of the depression, for most the "good things in life" all had to be put on hold. So does this mean that in this case, the number three didn't play out as I've said it should? Well no.

First, as is the case with the COVID-19 lockdowns, around the world people had to be pretty *creative* and *adaptable* with plenty of *imagination* to survive the depression. And of course something like the depression deeply affected everyone's *emotions*.

From a more positive perspective, the number three had a very important role during the 1930s due to its major emphasis on creativity.

US President Roosevelt's "New Deal" born of great creativity helped many Americans survive the depression. And creative new 1930s technologies in film and radio played a major role by entertaining everyone and so helping distract them from their woes.

In addition, many new creations came into being including the first frozen foods, Nestles "White" chocolate, the first all-talking all-colour wide-screen movie, and the first air mail service across the Atlantic to name but a few.

So especially, but not only, the creativity associated with the number three was certainly very well represented in the 1930s.

1940s

World War II began in September, 1939, and continued until September, 1945. And number four's key word is construction, which was definitely the focus of the second half of the 1940s after the destruction resulting from World War II. However number four descriptors like practicality, application, extreme seriousness, and opposition would certainly apply to the first half, as well as the second part of the decade.

1950s

While officially there are no good numbers and no bad numbers, it all depends on whether or not you're living your life in harmony with the particular year's major number, especially in relation to your personal-year number. But if there was a good number, the very best would be five. And five is the number of progress, freedom, movement, travel, communication, and minor new beginnings.

And so let's look into the wonderful 1950s. And sure  there were smaller wars like that in Korea, but throughout history there've always been wars somewhere around the world. Have you ever stopped to think about that? And have you ever wondered why? And will the 2000s with its emphasis on peacemaking ultimately put an end to war? All worthy of some thought.

But generally, around the world the 1950s was a decade of renewal. Most things were back on their feet after the post-World War II reconstruction phase and globally life was positive with an abundance of freedom. It was a time of new beginnings for most people and most countries.

Oh and it was during the 1950s, with the war over, that tourism began as an industry in its own right. New markets and opportunities opened up with discount tours, package tours, hotel chains, resorts, and the airlines introduced an economy class in planes so those with a more modest travel budget could afford to fly. And the 1950s also saw the beginning of the Space Race with the launch of Sputnik 1 — that really is *travel* on a massive scale.

1960s

Now to the Swinging Sixties, flower-power, love-ins, and a revolution in social norms, with sit-ins protesting against injustice, discrimination, inequality, and the introduction of the Civil Rights Act of 1964. The 1960s also saw the blossoming of decolonization in Africa, which began the decade before.

And the number six? Six is about humanitarianism, love, harmony, truth, justice, domesticity, idealism, responsibility, and so on. It's also the number of the teacher and the carer or nurse. All of which described the 1960s perfectly.

Now to the 1970s

1970s

Apart from bell-bottom trousers and discos, of greater importance to the 1970s were a lot of technological innovations such as the first microprocessors, calculators, video games, and even the first word processor, with the launch in 1971 of the Wang 1200. It was also a time of major scientific insights including an understanding of solid-state physics.

In my field of environmental ethics, it was in the early 1970s that the world was introduced to the notion of a specific field of ethics dedicated to the environment. And moral philosopher, Peter Singer, published his international best-

seller *Animal Liberation*. The first Earth Day was celebrated in 1970, and the US National Environmental Policy Act, the Clean Air Act, and the Clean Water Act all came into being in the 1970s.

The 1970s also saw the research into the activities of President Nixon, leading to his resignation from office. And it was during the 1970s that the so-called Spiritual New Age movement began.

And so it should be no surprise that the number seven is said to represent understanding, science, investigation, research and discovery, and perfection. It's also the number associated with spirituality, and New Age-type modalities.

1980s

The number eight is the number of money — either making it, losing it, or not having it. It's also the number of business, world-affairs, power-over, and authority.

And the catch-phrase for the 1980s has to be "Greed is Good" — thanks to Gordon Gecko and the 1987 film *Wall Street*. And October, 1987 also saw a major global stock market crash. *Oh why didn't we learn!*

It was a time marked by the start of globalization, and the technologies of the seventies leading to significant socio-economic changes. However developing countries experienced severe debt crises leading to a dependence on foreign aid. It was 1985 that the Live Aid concert was held to raise money for those starving in Ethiopian.

It's not hard to see the correlations between the number eight and the events in the 1980s. And so on to the 1990s.

1990s

As our system of numbers just runs from one to nine before repeating again in some form, nine is the number of completion. It generally contains the energetic vibrations of aspects of all the previous eight numbers. As such it can be a time of confusion and a combination of many things. But most importantly, it's the number of endings.

In addition it's a number of philanthropy, wisdom, and the preparation for the new beginning with the number one which follows, starting the new 1-9 cycle again.

And in the 1990s there was a rise in multiculturalism, the start of gene therapy, an end to world communism, and the Belfast "Good Friday" Agreement of 1998 saw an end to the conflict in Northern Ireland, which was also known as "The Troubles".

And it was 1989 that the worldwide web was developed, but on April 30th, 1993 it was introduced into the public domain. Throughout the 1990s, the World Wide Web continued to grow in preparation for the major part the Internet, email, and social media would have in our lives in the new millennium. It's the Internet, and its associated programs that play such a significant role in helping the rise of cosmic feminine-energy activities come to fruition.

If you're still sceptical about the numbers, just remember what I said in Chapter 4 about the quantum theory of global consciousness offering, at least, a plausible explanation of how the numbers, such as the two in the 2000s, might indeed influence global events. And remember too, the ridicule that Einstein received for some really wild theories like parallel lines crossing, and light coming to us in little packets of energy. Yet it's all true.

Appendix B: Significant Events in 2018

I n this appendix you'll find a list of just some of the many examples of the rise in the feminine and decline in negative masculine-energy that happened in 2018 alone.

Not only does this list reveal the speed with which these changes were occurring, but it's also an indication of the sorts of changes to watch out for in your own world in the future.

Also you'll recall the adage about ethics that I gave to all of my MBA students.

Ethical actions can often entail short-term pain, but will always result in long-term gains.

By contrast, unethical actions frequently have short-term gains, which make them so attractive.

But I guarantee that unethical actions will always result in some form of long-term pain and ultimate collapse, frequently in unexpected ways.

As you read through the following list, I invite you to reflect on how that adage has played out in many of the events below.

On a societal level in Australia alone in 2018 we saw numerous rejections of what were previously accepted, as opposed to acceptable, negative masculine-energy-based practices. Following are just a few of them.

❖ A Royal Commission investigating our banking and financial industry was held in Australia. A Royal Commission is the highest level of public inquiry, commissioned by the government, into the questionable actions of institutions. A bit like an American Congressional Hearing.

What are almost unbelievably unethical business practices were exposed with executives rightly losing their jobs. The underpinning issue is mainly associated with the various banks and financial institutions putting profits at all costs before the people they are in business to serve. Definitely a case of Me not We. The following are but three of numerous examples that were exposed on almost a daily basis.

1. Time and time again it was common practice to force high interest loans on vulnerable people who couldn't afford to meet the repayments and so the "victim" ended up bankrupt, homeless, and destitute, while the banks were still able to recoup their money.

2. Staff were bullied by management into meeting "sales" targets. And just to meet their targets some staff members regularly opened fraudulent bank accounts in the names of non-existent children.

3. But the worst one to come to light was the regular practice of continuing to charge people substantial fees for services that had not been supplied. And what was even worse was that these service fees continued to be charged for years after the person had died. Clearly there was no delivery of service there either.

I have no doubt these same practices are happening world-wide. It's the unethical "Big Short" approach to business all over again. Maybe it's time for a "Royal Commission" or its equivalent, into the banking and financial industry in your country too.

❖ At the end of March, 2018, in the game of cricket at an International level, we saw what used to be the all too common practice of ball-tampering.

The interesting part of this story is that in the past, if a player was caught doing this, he might be suspended for a match or two. This time however, the Australian public were so outraged that all three players involved, including one of the best cricketers in Australian *history*, were all removed from the game completely, in disgrace, for 12 months.

It was out-dated negative masculine-energy that was behind the need to win the International cricket "competition" no matter what, including the unethical practice of cheating. It was positive ethical feminine-energy that rose up like a tsunami throughout the Australian public saying "enough is enough" — this is no longer acceptable.

❖ That same tsunami of positive ethical feminine-energy led to the public saying "enough is enough" with regard to many other societal issues such as the Royal Commission into Institutional Responses to Child Sexual Abuse. That inquiry led to the criminal conviction of an Archbishop and the ultimate conviction of Cardinal George Pell, the world's third most senior member of the Catholic Church, just two levels below the Pope.

❖ Meanwhile on May 9th, 2018, the people of Malaysia elected 92-year-old, Mahathir Mohamad, as Prime Minister due to his promise to clean-up corruption that included the prosecution of the previous PM for allegedly stealing billions from the public-purse. The corruption was definitely negative masculine-energy in action, while the people of Malaysia supported the ethical, positive feminine-2-energy promise of Mahathir to clean up the corruption.

❖ Interestingly in early 2018 Kim Jong-un, the Supreme Leader of North Korea, softened his very negative masculine/military stance. It seemed to begin when he sent his *sister* with their team of athletes to the Winter Olympic Games in South Korea in February, 2018. Later he agreed to peace talks with the United States. Unfortunately, those talks became an on-again, off-again, affair for very questionable reasons. But it's a fascinating situation to watch, even today.

❖ In 2017, in my book, *Together, We CAN Change the World*, I wrote a very scathing section warning anyone wanting to change the world not to use Facebook as their source of credible information. And it was March, 2018, that the world began learning about the unethical Facebook activities leading to Mark Zuckerberg ending up before a US Congressional Hearing and on-going changes to the way Facebook is run. Although they still have a very long way to go.

❖ After only seven weeks as leader of her party, in late 2017 New Zealand elected as Prime Minister the most amazing example of positive feminine-2-energy in action—37-year-old, Jacinda Ardern. Shortly after being elected she announced that she was pregnant and her life-partner would become a stay-at-home dad while she ran the country. The baby was born in June, 2018. Prime Minister Ardern is the most laid-back, unassuming person you could possibly find and certainly the most inspirational and conscious leader I've ever come across.

❖ However in closing the list for some of the amazing 2018 events, it was the *aftermath* of this next very tragic event that made my heart sing the loudest.

You'll recall that back in the 1980s when I wrote my "Power of Two" paper I said the really exciting time would be from about 2022 for many reasons. Not the least of which would be because the babies born in and around the year 2000 and beyond would be reaching adulthood. And these young people born with this number two positive feminine-energy vibration would say "enough is enough" to so many things—the world has got to change. And around 2022, these young people will be getting to the age to make those changes happen.

But we didn't have to wait until 2022, because what happened on February 14th, 2018? Yet another senseless mass shooting occurred, this time at the Majory Stoneman Douglas High School in Parkdale, Florida. Seventeen people were killed. This led high school students throughout America to protest against the anachronistic US gun-laws saying "enough is enough", we deserve to be safe in our schools.

And when were these wonderful young high school students born? Shortly after the year 2000. Yes, like Greta Thunberg they are Gen Zs.

They might not have been old enough to vote, but they do have their social media skills that gives them a very loud voice. And female, male, and non-binary alike, they've been born with these inherent conscious positive feminine-2-*energy* characteristics that are insisting on a change to a more peaceful and loving world. There can be no clearer example of my 1980s forecasts coming to fruition than this one.

I invite you to just keep looking for those common patterns, themes, and trends in your local region, globally, and also as you watch or listen to the evening news. Keep asking yourself is this event an example of the rise in feminine-energy, or negative masculine-energy in its death-throes—or just a world gone mad? And if you think it's just a world gone mad; I invite you to take a deeper look for what might be hidden.

You'll recall the words of Phaedrus ~

Things are not always what they seem; the first appearance deceives many; the intelligence of a few perceives what has been carefully hidden.

Appendix C:
Events in 2019

In this appendix you'll find a short list of some of the more significant trends in 2019 demonstrating the rise in feminine-energy, the death-throes of negative masculine-energy, or both.

Although there will be times when I can't resist making a comment; for the most part, in this following list of noteworthy events[40], I'll let you do the work and decide which were the negative aspects and which were positive, and why.

❖ Throughout the entire year there was an on-again/off-again bromance between President Donald Trump and the Supreme Leader of North Korea Kim Jong-un. One day they're the best of friends with President Trump actually walking on North Korean soil, which was amazing. The next minute Kim is again letting off more rockets.

Now April was a big month for arguably positive reasons, even though some of the events have a negative foundation.

❖ Only a few weeks after the shocking Christchurch Mosque Massacre that left 51 people dead, the New Zealand parliament voted to ban military-style semi-automatic weapons. Yet America still can't do it, despite their shocking annual death-toll due to gun violence.

❖ After the newly-appointed Prime Minister of Ethiopia, Abiy Ahmed, promised to clean up the politics in his country, fifty-nine Ethiopian officials were arrested for corruption and economic sabotage. Six months later, in October, Prime Minister Abiy Ahmed was awarded the Nobel Peace Prize for helping end his country's 20-year war with Eritrea.

❖ On April 16, Egypt passed constitutional changes that could allow current President Sisi to rule until 2030. The changes also give Sisi more judiciary power. A great example of doing whatever it takes to cling to power — the death-throes of negative masculine-energy.

❖ Yet on the other side of the Atlantic, the former President of Peru, Alan Garcia, took his own life shortly before his arrest for money laundering and bribery.

❖ On a brighter and more bizarre note, the comedian Volodymyr Zelenskiy was elected President of Ukraine with 73.22% of the vote. Although he does have a law degree, his only political experience is playing a parody president on his TV show, "Servant of the People". So who knows, maybe it's Alec Baldwin for President in 2020!

❖ In May, Taiwan became the first Asian country to legalize same-sex marriage. And by the way, the national leader of Taiwan is a woman, Tsai Ing-wen.

❖ Also in May, South Africa made history when it was revealed that more than half the government's cabinet members were women.

❖ After many allegations of sexual misconduct, in July, the Canadian government agreed to pay $1 billion to members of the Armed Forces and National Defense, although, I must add, not admitting responsibility.

❖ And in August, Walmart who was responsible for 2% of US gun sales, announced a major change to their gun policy after a multiple shooting at Walmart's Texas store, and the death of two staff members at a Mississippi branch. Gun sales — very negative masculine-energy. The response to the new policy was very positive conscious feminine-2-energy.

After these policy changes, Walmart's shares immediately rose to an all-time high. So who is really running the US government, when in a democracy the government is just there to carry out the wishes of the majority of the people? And yet the US still hangs on to their anachronistic gun laws when clearly the majority of Americans want change. Talk about negative masculine-1-energy hanging on in its death-throes.

❖ And keeping the best till last, on December 9, 2019, Finland elected Sanna Marin as Prime Minister. Not only another female PM, but born in 1985, she's a Millennial and now the world's youngest head of government.

Endnotes

Because so many endnotes contain complex website addresses, to make it easier for people reading the paperback version to access those addresses, you'll find a copy of these endnotes at

https://www.consciouschangetoday.com/cct-endnotes/

1   The greatest change I made after hearing Johnny Manuel's performance was to change the title of what I'd published as *Conscious Feminism* to this book, *Conscious Change Today*. I also needed to tweak some of the original contents and add three new chapters to broaden my message. This change in title was because the title, *Conscious Feminism,* was one I was never comfortable with for many reasons, not the least of which is that my very important message was being sent to too narrow an audience.

2 Craig Kielburger August 15th, 2019
   https://kielburgerquotes.com/craig/589/

3 The *Doctrine of the Mean* is based on a cardinal rule that states: "... right conduct is incompatible with an excess or a deficiency in feelings and actions". *Nicomachean Ethics (NE)* NE. 1104a11-15

4 NE. 1106b9-20

5 Aristotle, NE. 1125b25-30

6   Stephen Juan, Ph.D. (2006) What are the most widely practiced religions of the world?
   https://www.theregister.co.uk/2006/10/06/the_odd_body_religion/

7   Julie Beck, 2018, The New Age of Astrology, *The Atlantic Daily* .
   https://www.theatlantic.com/health/archive/2018/01/the-new-age-of-astrology/550034/

8   Julie Beck, 2018, The New Age of Astrology, *The Atlantic Daily* .
   https://www.theatlantic.com/health/archive/2018/01/the-new-age-of-astrology/550034/

9   Laszlo, 2016—Laszlo, Ervin. 2016. "Consciousness Is Mind Beyond Space and Time: The New Paradigm". In Laszlo, Houston, and

Dossey. *What is Consciousness?* New Paradigm Books. New York: Select Books, Inc

[10] Stephen A. Russell, 2018. "The Order of Time: Carlo Rovelli's latest ideas will melt your brain"
https://thenewdaily.com.au/entertainment/books/2018/05/26/carlo-rovelli-the-order-of-time/?utm_source=Adestra&utm_medium=email&utm_campaign=Sunday%20Best%2020180527

[11] Dean Radin, 2009, *The Conscious Universe: The Scientific Truth of Psychic Phenomena*. Reprint edition. HarperOne.

Radin discusses global consciousness and details a number of these experiments and their results. See also The Global Consciousness Project, created originally in the Princeton Engineering Anomalies Research Lab at Princeton University, and is directed by Roger Nelson. http://noosphere.princeton.edu/

Plus The Institute of Noetic Sciences- https://noetic.org/

and the HeartMath Institute that conducts extensive studies in this field under the name of Global Interconnectedness and the Global Coherence Initiative see
https://www.heartmath.org/category/articles-of-the-heart/global-interconnectedness/

[12] Radin, 2009:187-188 — Radin, Dean. 2009. *The Conscious Universe: The Scientific Truth of Psychic Phenomena*. Reprint edition. HarperOne

[13] This website https://www.heartmath.org/resources/news-and-tools/# offers a range of free resources on Global Coherence and the effects of electromagnetic frequencies.

[14] McGilchrist, 2009 — McGilchrist, Iain. 2009. *The Master and His Emissary: The Divided Brain and the Making of the Western World*. Yale University Press

[15] David Cooperrider (as interviewed by Gotches & Ludema, 1995:6,8), the developer of Appreciative Inquiry describes it as a philosophy, a methodology, and also an intervention theory. He contends: "The aim of appreciative inquiry is to generate new knowledge which expands 'the realm of the possible' and helps the members of an organisation to envision a collectively desired future and to design improved organisational systems and processes that successfully translate their intentions into reality, and beliefs into practice". Greg Gotches, and Jim Ludema. 1995. "An Interview with David

Cooperrider on Appreciative Inquiry and the Future of OD".
Organizational Development Journal 13:5-13

[16] "I'm as mad as hell and I'm not going to take this anymore" was the catch-cry of Howard Beale, the lead character in the 1976 movie *Network*, which won four Academy Awards. Beale was a TV news anchor who was fed up with the corrupt practices of the TV networks and the crazy situation the world was in at the time. Sadly nothing has changed. And so one night Beale said on camera to the viewers in New York and the sixty-seven affiliated stations around the country; if they too were angry about the corruption and the world going crazy hurting so many people, they should go and fling open their window and yell out at the top of their voice: "I'm as mad as hell and I'm not going to take this anymore". This they did. But then they just went back inside and continued watching TV and so things continued on the same. This brilliant 5-minute video taken from the film is worth a look, even if you've seen the movie.
https://www.youtube.com/watch?v=AS4aiA17YsM

[17] http://www.youtube.com/watch?v=wjvq23sPrHA This video was made at 11am on October 10th, 2012. Four hours later Amanda killed herself. Search You Tube for "Amanda Todd's Final Video (4 Hours Before Death) | Unseen Footage (ORIGINAL) TheWeirdSidee"

[18] All the figures in this section were fact checked and contained in the ABC Science Unit article ~ Werner & Lyons. 2020. "The size of Australia's bushfire crisis captured in five big numbers".
https://www.abc.net.au/news/science/2020-03-05/bushfire-crisis-five-big-numbers/12007716

[19] It's worth investigating the website of Architect and Engineers for 911 — http://www.ae911truth.org/

[20] Search on You Tube for "JIM ROGERS - 8 Jun 2017 - Markets Crash By Late 2018-2019 You'll Know It", where he gives a number of reasons why the next crash will be far worse than that in 2007-2009.
https://www.youtube.com/watch?v=fdYXGhY4Dpk&index=9&list=PL4-7P201nd64gJ9OChMWcEtMwoZZmdFEm&t=10s

[21] Moore, 2016 — Moore, Michael. 2016. "Part 1: Michael Moore on Donald Trump, Bernie Sanders, and Brexit" October 6, 2016. 13.12m
https://www.youtube.com/watch?v=u7mweXE5RWE&t=299s

[22] Our Negativity Bias is an evolutionary trait that humans have wherein we place far more emphasis and focus on anything negative rather than seeking out the positive. I've explained it in more detail in my book, *Conscious Intelligence Competencies*.

23 Ruether, Rosemary Radford. 1975. *New Woman New Earth: Sexist Ideologies and Human Liberation*. New York: Seabury Press p204.

24 Juno Jordan. 1965/1978. *Numerology: The Romance in your Name*. Santa Barbara: J.F. Rowny Press; Faith Javance & Dusty Bunker. 1979/1986. *Numerology and The Divine Triangle*. Gloucester.MA: Para Research Inc.; John Arthur Daley. Nd. *Learning Numerology: Adventurer in Awareness*.

25 Aristotle's, *Nicomachean Ethics* — NE. 1142a01-20.

26 Aristotle, NE: 1125b25-30

27 Ford, Clementine. 2018. Interviewed on Late Night Live. Australian ABC Radio National. April, 26th, 2018.

28 Doyle, Kate, RG. Levtov, G. Barker, GC. Bastian, JB. Bingenheimer, S. Kazimbaya, et al. 2018. "Gender-transformative Bandebereho couples' intervention to promote male engagement in reproductive and maternal health and violence prevention in Rwanda: Findings from a randomized controlled trial". PLoS ONE 13:4. e0192756. https://doi.org/10.1371/journal.pone.0192756

29 See my book *Conscious Economic Sustainability* , (available shortly on Amazon).

30 As quoted in *Moving Forward: A Programme for a Participatory Economy*, by Michael Albert (2001:128). A slight variation, which appeared almost fifty years earlier was Capitalism is "the astonishing belief that the nastiest motives of the nastiest men somehow or other work for the best results in the best of all possible worlds". This was attributed to Keynes by Sir George Schuster in *Christianity and Human Relations in Industry*, 1951:109

31 Keynes, 1933; republished in Collected Works Vol. 11 (1982)

32 The term Environmental Affirmative Action and also Ecological Affirmative Action was one I coined in the 1990s when I was working on my PhD.

33 Global Footprint Network, 2016 — *The Living Planet Report* is published each year by the Global Footprint Network. http://www.footprintnetwork.org/pt/index.php/GFN/page/living_planet_report2/

34 Massey and Hamilton, 2012. Choice Point is now available for free viewing at http://www.choicepointmovement.com/free-movie

35 *Choice Point: Align Your Purpose* (2012 Video)-Plot Summary — http://www.imdb.com/title/tt2615982/plotsummary?ref_=tt_ov_pl

[36] Tyler, Patrick, 2003. "Threats and Responses: News Analysis; A New Power In The Streets". *The New York Times*. February 17, 2003. http://www.nytimes.com/2003/02/17/world/threats-and-responses-news-analysis-a-new-power-in-the-streets.html

[37] Deen, Thalif. 2005. "'New Superpower' Seeks 'Better World'". June 3, 2005. Politics: Inter Press Service New Agency. http://ipsnews.net/news.asp?idnews=28943

[38] NE. 1106b9-20

[39] Appreciative Inquiry is a relatively new positive change process that builds on the things that are currently working and dismisses problems that aren't working as opposed to trying to solve them. David Cooperrider (as interviewed by Gotches & Ludema, 1995:6), the developer of Appreciative Inquiry describes it as a philosophy, a methodology, and also an intervention theory. He contends: "The aim of appreciative inquiry is to generate new knowledge which expands 'the realm of the possible' and helps the members of an organisation to envision a collectively desired future and to design improved organisational systems and processes that successfully translate their intentions into reality and beliefs into practice". (Cooperrider in Gotches & Ludema, 1995:8)

[40] I thank the website https://www.infoplease.com/2019-current-events for reminding me of so many of these events.

Kashonia's Story

Dr. Kashonia Carnegie
PhD; MSc; MA; BA (Hons)

Conscious Change Ethicist
Moral Philosopher
Conscious Change Consultant

I've lived a very colourful life, both personally and professionally. And although I've worked and travelled extensively overseas, I was born and have lived my entire life in Australia.

In my 20s, I raised day old calves on a little farm in Central New South Wales; set up and ran several small businesses; and lived under the stars with my two dogs, Freddie and Samson, in Australia's harsh Outback. In the Outback I caught wild donkeys and trucked them to sanctuaries in Brisbane to prevent them from being killed as vermin.

Following a move to Melbourne, which was a *major* culture shock, I was appointed Australia's first female oil company representative where my duties were those of a business coach long before the term "business coach" was ever even thought of. I also based that coaching work exclusively on conscious business and conscious leadership strategies, before the "conscious" label was ever thought of. And the results could not have been better.

It was during my 30s that I had yet another major career change spending the next 14 years working in the media, primarily as a talk-back radio broadcaster. During that time, I won the radio industry's Pater award for the best voice on Australian radio due to what were my conscious communication skills.

However, while I was on Melbourne's radio 3AW, despite having left school in 9th grade at the age of 15, the opportunity arrived to do some special entry exams for a mature-aged placement as a 1st year undergraduate university student. This was the start of a decade plus of academic studies with majors in Moral Philosophy, Peace Studies, Environmental Philosophy, philosophy-based Applied Ethics, Environmental Management and Environmental Education. My PhD thesis/dissertation focused on what is now known as the ethics of conscious change and was called *Heart-Centred Virtue Ethics: Raising Ecological Consciousness in Organisations.*

I went on to teach ethics, leadership skills, and change management, based on conscious intelligence competencies, for the MBA programs at a couple of leading universities in Australia and their off-shore campuses in Hong Kong and Singapore.

During that time, I also spent a couple of years delivering an Ecotourism Interpretation workshop that I designed for the Singapore National Parks Board which was held in the beautiful National Parks in Singapore. And as many of my classes were held in the open, my "students" often included the macaque monkeys who joined in while watching intently from the trees above.

Woven throughout all of my media and university work were extensive academic and independent studies in areas such as spirituality, religious studies, quantum theory, systems theory, creativity, positive psychology, coaching psychology, neuroscience, and behavioural science including Practitioner and Master Practitioner levels of NLP (Neuro-Linguistic Programming). These studies were combined with a range of different work activities as a leadership coach, corporate trainer, speaker, and also sessional mediator/conciliator for the Department of Justice in the Australian states of Victoria and Queensland.

My greatest passion is to elicit the magic in others that enables them to manifest boundaryless possibilities leading to their transformation into conscious leaders of change; so that they too can, in turn, transform into conscious leaders everyone they connect with, resulting in us all working to create a truly conscious world of peace, love, and sustainability.

Acknowledgements

Judith Sherven PhD, and Jim Sniechowski PhD, Judith & Jim, whose kindness, compassion, and support have changed my life on more than one occasion.
https://judithandjim.com/

Ryan Eliason whose loving and sensitive heart and yet pragmatic intellect showed me how to turn a range of disparate save-the-world passions and ideas into a cohesive business plan. https://ryaneliason.com/

Geoff Affleck whose brilliant right-brain creativity coupled with his left-brain knowledge of the book marketing world taught me the most effective way to bring my many books to the world. https://geoffaffleck.com/

Made in the USA
Middletown, DE
14 December 2020